A CHILD'S PURSUIT OF ART

BROWN **ART SERIES**

Consulting Editor WILLARD F. WANKELMAN
Bowling Green State University
Bowling Green, Ohio

for Amy, Eric, Heidi,
and our mothers and fathers

Amy Jane Herberholz: felt tip pen drawing.
From the collection of the authors.

A CHILD'S PURSUIT OF ART

110 MOTIVATIONS FOR DRAWING, PAINTING, AND MODELING . . . . .

Donald W. Herberholz
Sacramento State College

Barbara J. Herberholz
Art Teacher and Photographer

WM. C. BROWN COMPANY PUBLISHERS
Dubuque, Iowa

Printed in U. S. A.

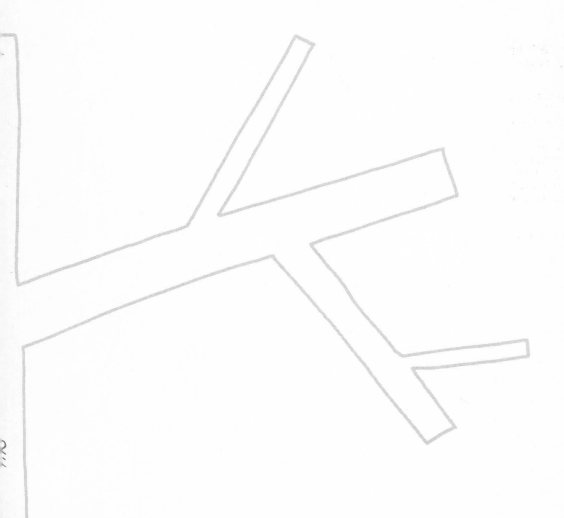

Acknowledgments

The authors gratefully acknowledge the co-operation of the following persons and organizations for the help they gave in the total process of organizing the material in this book: Corrine Geeting, the Sacramento Country Day School, Joyce Witt, Alice Soderberg, Ed Larson, Helen Bradfield, Sister Claudine, St. Ignatius School, Robert Ulmer, Dr. Ralph Tippin, Ralph Talbert, DeWitt Jayne, Sharon Corcoran, George Nicks, Donna Bangs, Kathryn Mills, Mission School, the San Juan Unified School District, and last but not least, the neighborhood children who modeled for the photographs. We are indebted to the book companies and museums for their permission to reproduce and quote the items as noted throughout the book.

Foreword

Children have been in pursuit of art ever since they invented it millenniums ago. Adults, however, are the only ones who occupy themselves with the attempts of trying to explain it; children neither want nor try to explain. The futility of the attempts to explain art was never more convincingly expressed than it was by Picasso who, when asked for an explanation of art, replied, "How can you explain the song of a bird?"

Children's art is the immediate and instantaneous expression of children's relationships with the world around them. The immediacy and poignancy of the expressions are their own satisfying rewards; the simplicity or complexity of them are of little or no consequence. What is important to children, and eventually to adults, is the manifest involvement and enjoyment of art as it assumes multivarious forms from infanthood to maturity.

A Child's Pursuit of Art is the result of a decade or more of concentrated effort by a highly coordinated team of exceptional art educators (and their children), Donald and Barbara Herberholz, to provide immediate and proven means by which children everywhere may be guided into continuing and expanding involvement in the visual arts. Simultaneously, it provides salient means by which parents and teachers may find positive ways with which to reinvest those children's interests in the rewarding psychological and pragmatic experiences of art who have been deliberately or inadvertently diverted from it.

The authors make it clear that the time is now. The place is our own home, school or neighborhood and the whole interesting and infinitely stimulating world around it. The children are our own, the neighbor's, or the total school population in the hamlet, town or metropolitan area. The means are there for the asking and using, and the rewards of overwhelming scope will be both real and implied, immediate and far-reaching, intimately personal and at the same time universal.

Fundamental to the design of the multitudinous art experiences available to all are the acts of perception that enable man to have transactions with the amazing, concrete world around him. Coupled with these acts of perception are flights of imagination projecting images from within and integrating compatible ones into unusual and often unique forms that announce a moment of creation. Something new has been made! No experience available to man provides a more exciting and satisfying identity with the felt forces of the universe than those when an individual evolves a form of his own fashioning. Let us see. Let us touch. Let us listen, run, lift, pull and push. Come, let us create!

ALEXANDER MASLEY

Chairman, Department of Art Education
The University of New Mexico

Introduction

Motivation for creativity and self-expression is not always an easy task. Thus this book is planned and designed to aid the teacher, the prospective teacher, and the parent in understanding and implementing their basic method of developing aesthetic responses in the elementary school children. It is primarily a source of ideas for art expression in the school, home, or any environment in which children are encouraged and given freedom to express their ideas through art materials.

Depending on the age level of the child and on his past experiences in art, the teacher or parent may use any part or all of a motivation as it is written. In the main, the motivations are not limited to any one art material. The process of creation and expression may be carried out with any number of materials or procedures, both two- and three-dimensional. The motivations are so constructed as to challenge the pupil and to cause him to become personally absorbed in the ideas presented. The motivational dialogues set the stage for the child to discover his own individual potential through art expression.

Divergent paths are listed at the end of each sub-category to inspire additional motivational ideas in the adult and to aid him in conceiving and building dialogues which he can use in guiding the children's art expression.

Photographs to heighten awareness, to stimulate thinking, and to aid and encourage the adult in a more intense identification with children's experiences are presented in depth and from many points of view throughout the text.

Reproductions of works of well-known artists are used in conjunction with a number of the motivations to indicate that both the adult artist and the child have experiences in common which can be readily expressed in art forms.

Table of Contents

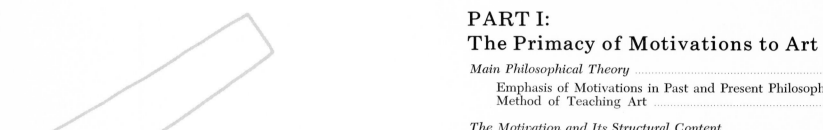

PART I:
The Primacy of Motivations to Art

THE FOREST
A child's painting from the collection of the authors.

* Creating and expressing one's own thoughts, feelings, and perceptions with imagination, sensitivity, and skill is the most important aim in the elementary art program.

Every properly functioning human being transforms the visual signals that he receives from outside into structured, meaningful entities. Without the perceptual ordering of his sense response into images of things in space, man cannot orient himself. Without shaping his physical environment in accordance with these images, he cannot survive. His capacity to structure his environment according to his needs — that is, his ability to work out a rapport with his world — determines the quality of his life.

Gyorgy Kepes
from EDUCATION OF VISION
Copyright 1965 by George Braziller, Inc., New York
Reprinted by permission of George Braziller, Inc.
New York: George Braziller, Inc.
1965, page i

PART I:

The Primacy

of

Motivations

to Art

Motivate — induce, move, draw on, give an impulse to, inspire, prompt, stimulate, inspirit, rouse, arouse, animate, incite, provoke, instigate

Main Philosophical Theory

Art education practices for the past two decades have been firmly founded on the philosophy that the child has the innate capacity to transform the primary means of knowing, that is, his experiences of *feeling, thinking,* and *perceiving,* into his own unique art forms. In attempting to retain and foster the precious human gift of discovery through art, leading art education authorities have emphasized the importance and value of motivations as the primary method of evoking art responses in the child.

＊Art is one of man's basic drives. Each and every civilization has had its art forms from the day that some prehistoric man picked up a stick and scratched in the sand or painted on his cave wall, to the highest forms achieved by the Egyptians, the Renaissance artists, and the present day men and women who interpret our world with paint, ink, torch, or chisel.

Children begin to scribble as naturally as they begin to babble and, if uninterrupted, continue to develop expressive visual forms.

Emphasis of Motivations in Past and Present Philosophy

Beginnings of motivations in art as they are understood today had their roots in the teachings of Franz Cizek[1] in Austria at the turn of the century and later in the teachings of Natalie Cole[2] in the United States. More recent writers including Lowenfeld and Brittain,[3] Mendelowitz,[4] Keiler,[5] Mattil,[6] Wankelman,[7] Jefferson,[8] McFee,[9] Linderman and Herberholz,[10] Conrad,[11] Wachowiak and Ramsay,[12] Gaitskell,[13] and others continue to emphasize in their art education philosophy the responsibility of parents and teachers in providing motivations for the young child. Thus, it is the responsibility — and the privilege — of teachers and parents to furnish the stimulation needed by the child to induce him to reach into the wellsprings of his inner self, into his primary experiences, to find there some happenings that excited his interest strongly enough for him to want to express them as visualized configurations.

Through acting-it-out during a motivation, children crystallize their feelings and ideas which they then express in picture form. The general background for their concepts comes from previous happenings and perceptual experiences. These form the wellsprings of art.

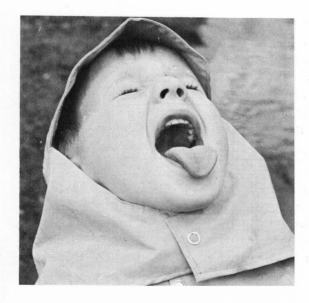

To instill such attitudes by teaching requires something more than the mere presentation of fundamental ideas. Just what it takes to bring off such teaching is something on which a great deal of research is needed, but it would seem that an important ingredient is a sense of excitement about discovery — discovery of regularities of previously unrecognized relations and similarities between ideas, with a resulting sense of self-confidence in one's abilities.

Jerome S. Bruner
from THE PROCESS OF EDUCATION
Cambridge, Mass.: Harvard University Press
1960, p. 20

Method of Teaching Art

Teaching art by the motivational method presents to the child an opportunity to crystallize concrete forms from impressions received, ideas conceived, and experiences lived. When an art period follows a stimulating motivation, emotions, thoughts, and perceptions become integrated in the child. The deeper and more complete the integration, the faster will be the outpouring of the forms in the art product and the greater aesthetic quality it will have.

Well-structured motivation becomes the basic key to good art teaching in the elementary school. Many real and vicarious experiences in and out of school can be placed under the following motivational categories: Direct Happenings, Roundabout Happenings, Imagination Stretchers, Point-of-View Changers,[14] and Cluster Activities.

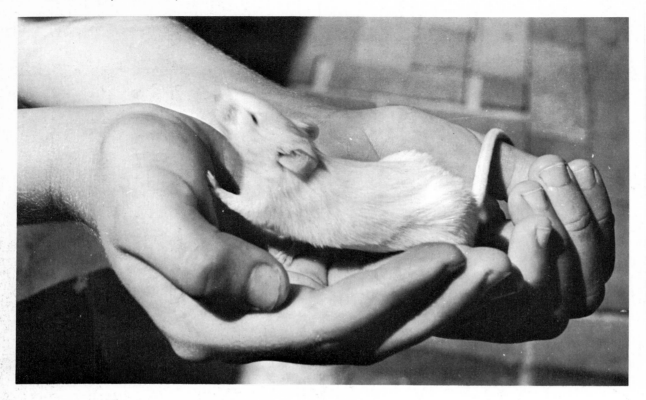

Seek greater depths in an experience or observation by digging deeper into its varied aspects.

Encourage the imagination to grope beyond the confines of the object or experience.

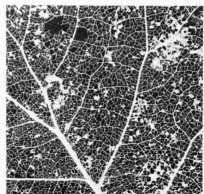

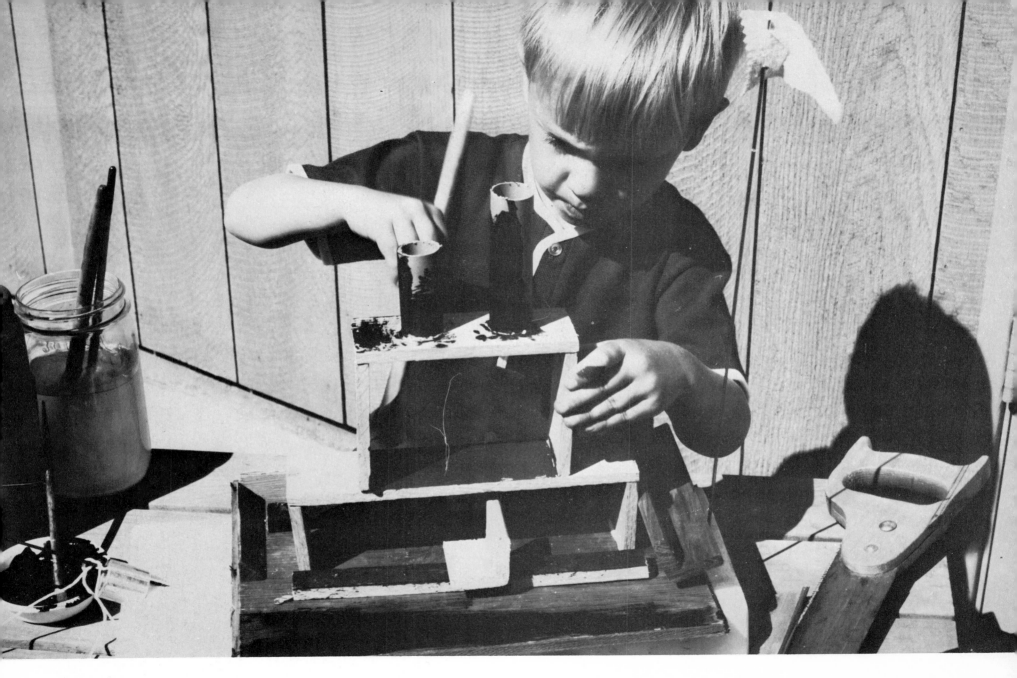

Through art activities emotions, thoughts and perceptions become integrated.

. . . . .it is precisely through the role of the teacher that the two elements of experimentation and reflection or analysis come together: the student works out his own ideas within the structure of a series of specific problems designed by the teacher to guide him to a clearer understanding of the whole spectrum of art forms past and present.

Zelda Dana Wirtschafter
from SEMINAR ON ELEMENTARY AND SECONDARY
SCHOOL EDUCATION IN THE VISUAL ARTS
Howard Conant, editor
New York: New York University Printing Office
1965, pp. 163-64

The Motivation and Its Structural Content

The child's pursuit of art emerges from a mingling of pre-verbal primary sensitivities, concrete experiences, and intuitive and aesthetic feelings coupled with a child's capacity to be puzzled. The articulate process of transformation of these perceptions into his personalized art forms may come about through a strong self-motivation or the teacher may help motivate the child to order his personalized detailed impressions.

Acting as a compass, the motivating force helps the child navigate in, around, and through his experiences (thoughts, feelings, and perceptions) with a deeper concentrated involvement, and thus he avoids the dangers of a barren or superficial visual response. In this type of self-involvement, the child is essentially engrossed in the technique of discovery[15] whereby he takes in information which he can check against his own ideas. He learns to manipulate his ideas, knowledge, and materials to solve new tasks that he has set for himself. He learns to unmask the commonplace events and to use them in unique ways. Through the motivation, he learns to nurture his aesthetic qualities and to let them unfold into spontaneous organized visual images, resulting in a highly personal, art expression.

Because the structure of the creative process[16] involved in art is essentially the same as that involved in other disciplines, the child is developing attitudes which will be of benefit to him in other research processes. An art motivation requires the child to look critically not only for meaning and details, but for the unusual and the uncommon. This training provides a broad base for other research areas which he may pursue later in life.

In summary, a motivation is:
A perception builder
A concept maker
An imagination stretcher
A perceptual heightener
A convergent-thinking developer
An emotion cultivator
A visual-image former
A divergent-thinking prodder
An idea-generating session

THE CIRCUS FERNANDO: THE RINGMASTER, Henri de Toulouse-Lautrec
Courtesy of: The Art Institute of Chicago
              The Joseph Winterbotham collection

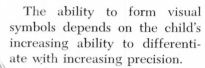

The ability to form visual symbols depends on the child's increasing ability to differentiate with increasing precision.

When a child looks at an object, don't tell him what it is or what it is used for, but direct his visual attention to the form, color, texture, and line qualities.

Photo Credit: Sharon Corcoran

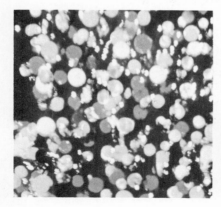

A work of art is an expressive form created for our perception through sense or imagination, and what it expresses is human feeling. The word "feeling" must be taken here in its broadest sense, meaning everything that can be felt, *from physical sensation, pain and comfort, excitement and repose, to the most complex emotions, intellectual tensions, or the steady feeling-tones of a conscious human.*

Susanne K. Langer
from PROBLEMS OF ART
New York: Charles Scribner's Sons
1957, page 15

Extending Aesthetic and Emotional Qualities Through Art Skills

Art in the elementary school must go beyond helping children express "something." It must aid them in expressing their aesthetic responses with increasing effectiveness and with some measure of artistic dimension. The skills which a child develops in responding to a motivation are essential tools for refining his art products. They may be considered skills in:

Selecting, setting, and solving problems
Selecting functional materials for appropriate expression
Inventing ideas
Using imagination and humor
Thinking divergently
Perceiving, portraying details, relationships, differences and
    similarities in color, function, shape, line, texture
Remembering a specific experience vividly and coherently

Each moment and each experience is a new wonder for the child. The happy task of the teacher or parent is to inspire young people to discover themselves and the world and to express their newly-found thoughts, feelings, and perceptions in art forms. From achievement and recognition springs confidence. A continuous pattern of experience-expression brings forth the blossom of aesthetic growth to full bloom.[17]

Art qualities must be encouraged because self-expression does not necessarily have art form.

To respond in a realistic sense means that I respond with my real human power, that of suffering, of joy, of understanding, to the reality of the "object" which experiences something. I respond to the person as he is; to the experience of the other person as it is. I respond not with my brain or my eyes or my ears. I respond as the whole person I am. I think with my belly. I see with my heart. When I respond to an object with the real powers in me, which are fitted to respond to it, the object ceases to be an object. I become one with it. I cease to be the observer. I cease to be the judge. This kind of response occurs in a situation of complete relatedness, in which seer and seen, observer and observed, become one, although at the same time they remain two.

Eric Fromm
from "The Creative Attitude"
CREATIVITY AND ITS CULTIVATION,
H. H. Anderson, editor
New York: Harper & Row
1959, p. 48

Motivations As Multisensory Experiences

The areas of the emotions and physical senses are meshed and intertwined with the thought processes. Provocative questions in a motivation comprise a system of inquiry which assists the child in ordering the scope and scale of new situations from various directions and view points. The motivation arouses questions which cause the child to reflect and to search for his own meaning that he will later reveal in his art.

Strength, richness, and order that unfold in the child's art product are highly related to the meaningful entities structured within the motivational questions. The probing thoughts in a motivation help a child cast about for his personal forms of feeling and visual thinking which, when clustered together, will help him search out the aesthetic structure he is trying to understand. He assembles new information during the motivational process to build a framework for a stronger structure and a deeper involvement into the substance of art. He becomes aware of a more highly developed aesthetic quality as he engages in a deeper dialogue between himself and his environment which ultimately emerges in his newly found visual forms. The well-structured motivation in its unfolding incites the child to pursue exciting new thoughts which he may incorporate in his artistic expression.

The child reflects and searches for his own meaning to be revealed in his art.

Children need pressure-free hours to become acquainted with themselves and their world, to explore it, to become sensitive to it.

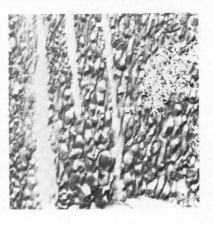

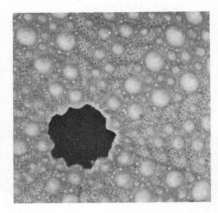

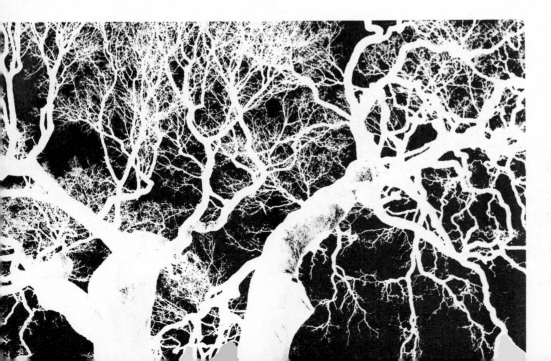

⚹ A way to help unite the barrage of sensory experiences is an art motivation in which many of the sensory impressions are brought into a more meaningful united whole.

No longer can we consider the artistic process as self-contained, mysteriously inspired from above, unrelated and unrelatable to what people do otherwise. Instead, the exalted kind of seeing that leads to the creation of great art appears as an outgrowth of the humbler and more common activity of the eyes in everyday life.

Rudolf Arnheim
from ART AND VISUAL PERCEPTION
Berkeley and Los Angeles: University of California Press
1965, p. viii

Maintaining the Motivational Dialogue

During a highly successful motivation, the teacher builds and maintains two dialogues. One dialogue is between the teacher and the child and the other is between the child's inner and outer experiences.

In order to assist the child in the pursuit of his personal dialogue, the teacher must be well versed in:

Leading the child to the edge or threshold of
discovery
Evoking the child's thoughts to brush up against
his emotions and intermingle with his sense
perceptions
Inducing, tempting, stimulating within the
child a clarification of his shadowy, vague,
emotional glimmerings so that they become felt strongly enough to burst forth
into art forms

The adult must also be aware that the motivational dialogues should:

Delay openness
Be rooted in a primary experience
Help the child focus on a detailed particular
Increase the child's capacity to wonder
Assist the child in exploring new ideas
Allow the child time to toy or play with an idea
Add the dimension of relatedness

Heighten inner reflections of the self
Leave open divergent paths for future con-
sideration
Stimulate imagination and humor[18]

In sum, then, the teacher's task as communicator, model, and identification figure can be supported by a wise use of a variety of devices that expand experience, clarify it, and give it personal significance. There need be no conflict between the teacher and the aids to teaching. There will be no conflict if the development of aids takes into account the aims and the requirements of the teacher.

Jerome S. Bruner
from THE PROCESS OF EDUCATION
New York: Vintage Books,
1960, p. 91

Provocative Vision-Building Words

Good motivation contains both structure and process, the content encompassing an area or several areas common to all the children in the class. Every motivation should be filled with emotion-packed words and feelings since the child uses emotions as one of his fundamental basis for expression. Time spent in motivating should be crackling w i t h excitement. Brightly-colored phrases aid the children in seeing and feeling more strongly so that they will respond with heightened creative expression.

This phase of motivation can materially aid the teacher or parent because of its challenge of supplying words to fit a specific sight, sound, or feeling. The child can be stimulated by being asked for a word or words to express reaction to the situation. This can crystallize the reaction of a child so that he can more readily express his interpretation through some art media.

A meaningful experience may appear directly or indirectly, days or weeks later in a drawing, painting, or modeling.

The forces that characterize the meaning of the story become active in the observer, and produce the kind of stirring participation that distinguishes artistic experience from the detached acceptance of information.

Rudolf Arnheim
from ART AND VISUAL PERCEPTION
Berkeley and Los Angeles: University of California Press
1965, p. 437

Measuring the Spirit and Strength of a Motivation

Illumination of the experience for the child should be accomplished by the structure[19] of the motivation. This can be instrumental in increasing his range of sensibilities and depth of feelings.[20] Structuring (or organization of a motivation) may therefore increase the capacity of a child to create visual forms more fluently and clearly. This phase is fundamental to the child's development of visualized forms.

Following the use of a motivational dialogue, the teacher or prospective teacher may want to reflect and decide upon its effectiveness. The Spirit and Strength Check List, given here, can materially aid in deciding the strengths and weaknesses of a motivation.

Spirit and Strength Check List

Did the motivation promote continued openness?

Did it have its roots in a primary experience?

Did it help the child focus on a detailed particular?

Did it include a dimension of self-identification in its structure?

Did it climax in crystallizing the ideas which evolved?

Did it develop or increase the capacity to wonder?

Did it assist the child in exploring new ideas?

Did it allow the child time to toy with an idea?

Did it sharpen the child's perception?

Did it employ colorful words and action-packed phrases?

Did it point out differences and similarities?

Did it allow the imagination to flow?

Did it heighten the inner reflection of the self?

Did it require non-verbal answers?

Did it encourage unusual and unexpected responses?

Did it allow for spontaneous eruptions from the child?

Children see and feel familiar relationships as much as they reach out for new ones when they dramatize a motion, handle real objects, listen for splendid sounds, and enthuse to exciting ideas.

The child creates fluently and clearly.

The teacher who only hands out materials, then leaves the children to "create" out of a vacuum, is surely not fulfilling his role, which is one of establishing a wholesome climate for creative work, providing good motivations, introducing sufficient orderly procedure to insure good basic foundations on which to work, and then permitting the child to use his own ideas for the development of his project.

Edward L. Mattil
from MEANING IN CRAFTS,
Second Edition
Prentice-Hall, Inc., Englewood Cliffs, N. J.
© 1965, p. 9
Reprinted by permission of Prentice-Hall, Inc.,
Englewood Cliffs, N. J.

Piloting a Motivation

In responding to a motivation, the child is challenged to reflect, to relate, and to form a variety of ideas. He is encouraged to be inventive, imaginative, and original. He is guided in exercising self-judgment and self-discipline as he discards, chooses, limits, and controls. His uniqueness as a person is recognized and valued, and this very *acceptance* removes the hindering barriers for a continuous on-going pattern of creative growth.

To judge success in a motivation, the teacher should first develop an awareness of the children's growing interest and excitement during the motivation itself. If questions and provocative ideas are stimulating, the children's mounting involvement can easily be felt. The alert teacher knows when the cut-off point of the motivational dialogue is reached and when further motivation might create restlessness because of the eagerness of the children to proceed with the art activity itself. Continuing of the motivation beyond the desirable cut-off point could cause definite loss of spontaneity and interest in some or all of the children. It may necessitate practice to develop this technique but it will be of considerable benefit in working with children of all age levels.

To steer and to stimulate the teacher in reviewing and re-informing and extending memories of things, happenings, places, people, and objects from the world of nature,[21] photographic cues are used throughout the book.

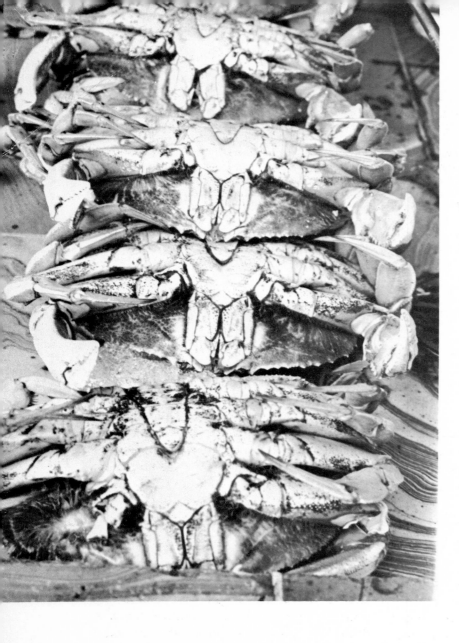

To differentiate the essential in an experience from the non-essential is highly subjective and varies with the individual artist.

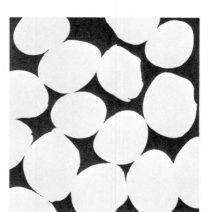

Transfer of training from one field to another does not take place automatically; but the use of principles, concepts, skills, and attitudes learned in one situation can be applied to other situations. To reinforce the children's transfer of learning between art and other subjects, direct references should be made, showing them how the same ability or organizational pattern operates in both situations. For example, children may have learned to look for design in art and outdoors, but may not see it when they look at things under a microscope. Show them that similar kinds of patterning are present. Help them look for the particular form of order and variation when they look at nature in finer detail. Children may be able to see design in abstract forms, but when they look at pictures of real things they are so concerned with the things that they fail to see the organization. Encourage them to look at the basic forms, lines, and colors. Sometimes looking at a picture upside down helps this transfer of training to take place — the things have to be set in an unreal position for the child to see the pattern.

June McFee
from PREPARATION FOR ART
Belmont, Calif.: Wadsworth Publishing Co., Inc.
1961, p. 228

Things to Remember: Motivational Practice

1. It is desirable for the teacher to have the materials ready and distributed before the motivation begins. He can let the children know what the choice of material is, the size of paper, and any other helpful information. It might be wise for the teacher to hold back one work item, such as the brushes, until the motivation is over. Then the remaining item can be distributed and the work can begin. This method prevents the children from "jumping the gun" and also avoids loss of "peak of excitement" if the materials have to be distributed after the motivation is presented.

2. It is essential for the teacher to have every child's attention before beginning the motivation.

3. The teacher must indicate enthusiasm and excitement about the topic. He should learn to use a *genuine* smile as he talks. To be most effective, a motivation should be presented by a person who has empathy, imagination, and enthusiasm not only for *children* but also for *art*. A brief study of the topic to be used will provide the teacher with self-confidence, and it will frequently aid him in presenting a more interesting motivation period.

4. The teacher can tell the children that many of the questions asked are to be answered *silently* by each child as each will have *different* answers, and there is usually no one

correct answer. If verbal answers are given to each question, the motivation will take so long that it will lose its impact. The silent answer will encourage individual interpretation of the subject by each child as he pours forth on paper his expression of the subject. *Some questions can of course be responded to verbally by the children, and some questions can't be answered with words since the answers deal with feelings and the children will need to use the lines, shapes, and colors in their pictures to tell what they experienced.*

5. It is important for the teacher to realize that the younger children need a shorter motivation time. The motivation time is gradually increased from younger to older age levels.

6. While the same general motivational topic may be used at all grade levels, the points to stress vary according to the age of the child and to his past creative art experiences. During kindergarten, first, and second grades, "I and my" are words that aid the child in a greater understanding of himself. The emotional appeal of a topic takes top priority in these early years; and, while questions dealing with the emotional feelings should still be included during third through sixth grades, the older youngster is ready to deal with questions pointed toward increasing and helping him express his visual awareness. Here the key words change to "we, where, how, when, and what action was involved." During these later years, the more involved visual and emotional space concepts, the inside and outside of objects, overlapping in nature, self-identification, size relationships, more conscious use of design qualities, and visual details of clothing and bodily movements gradually become integrated and absorbed in the child's artistic language.

7. After the children have been working for a short time, each child can be stimulated in the direction of his thinking. The teacher need not feel that a motivation has failed if interest lags for some children during the work period. Some youngsters need extra encouragement and need to be reminded of ideas previously discussed.

8. When the activity comes to an end, the completed art work is displayed, and the children can talk about their work basing the discussion on some of the points listed under Child's Check List on page 37.

9. Sporadic use of motivations will not cultivate sufficient growth in aesthetic responding. Regular times for art must be planned for and adhered to in the week's schedule.

10. It is recommended that the teacher show works of art by adult artists to the children. These are readily and abundantly available in the form of purchased prints, magazines, books, commercial collections, and from galleries. The black and white reproductions of paintings, drawings, and sculpture included in this book illustrate the common experiences of both the adult artist and the child.

THE BALLOON MAN
A child's painting from the collection of the authors.

Art is a means by which an individual tells others how he feels about his world.

And, above all, remember you are not trying to make your child an artist. It is his creativeness you care about: his sensitivity; originality; adaptability; fluency; flexibility; and the powers of synthesis, analysis, and redefinition. You can encourage all of these in his daily life. Some day, they may come home to roost in unexpected fields like medicine, business, law, or science, and you may have reason to be extraordinarily proud of that little boy or girl who sprawled on the living-room rug with a box of broken crayons filling large sheets of cheap paper with figments of childish imagination.

Viktor Lowenfeld
from Creativity: "Education Stepchild"
A SOURCE BOOK FOR CREATIVE THINKING
Edited by Sidney J. Parnes and Harold F. Harding
New York: Charles Scribner's Sons
1962, p. 16

Things to Remember: Control of Material

1. Materials should be easily accessible to avoid as much confusion and moving around the room as possible. In tempera painting, for instance, the children can be divided into groups of six or whatever number may be convenient for the specific class. The teacher can spread papers on the floor or on tables and can provide one set of colors with a brush in each jar of color for each group. A large can of water for washing a brush and some paper towels for drying them enables children to switch sizes of brushes as their painting needs demand. Small as well as large bristle brushes should be available. The teacher should remind the children that the first color must be dry before they paint another color on top of it or near it or both colors will blur together.

2. If a child prefers to outline his picture before he paints it with tempera, chalk is suggested as a suitable material for this purpose. A light crayon may be used for outlining or sketching in preparation for a crayon drawing.

3. In cut and torn paper work, the children can cut and tear freely without drawing the shapes first. Details should be added with more bits and pieces of colored paper rather than being drawn in with pencil lines.

4. The teacher can pre-mix some tempera colors. He can try adding white to some colors, black to others, mixing orange and yellow, red and blue, green and blue, or any desired combination to increase the children's awareness of variation in tone, light and dark, bright-

ness, how colors look when used next to other colors, in large amounts, and when repeated several times.

5. The teacher can occasionally limit the number of colors to be used in a drawing or painting to three or four with the choice of these colors determined by each individual child.

6. The wise teacher will think through the motivation and will try to select appropriate materials for the subject matter. For example, if the motivation is "I am doing exercises," the children can use clay[22] for this self-expression.

7. For variation, the teacher can vary the size, shape, and color of the paper. A long narrow paper or a square shape, for instance, tends to make for greater flexibility than the usual paper of 12″ x 18″ size. Black paper tends to make tempera paint sparkle. Colored paper gives unity and a feeling for a filled-in background.

8. A chunk of clay salt ceramic or prepared papier maché mix as large as a child's fist is an appropriate size to provide for each child for modeling. The teacher can give each child a square of corrugated cardboard, floor tile, or slab of wood upon which to work. A variety of tools should be available for shaping and texturing — such as toothpicks, nails, hairpins, orange sticks, spoons, combs, or any object that might create an interesting texture. Salt ceramic and papier maché pulp can be modeled over cores and armatures of wood, cardboard tubes, toothpicks, pipe cleaners, wires, etc.

9. Materials and their combinations should be varied regularly. This procedure tends to avoid monotony for the children. One can try:

> Felt tip pens
> Cut and torn colored paper
> Colored tissue paper and cloth collages
> Thick wax crayon and thin water color resists
> Painting with sticks, bits of sponges, Q-tips
> Painting on wet paper
> Oil crayons (Sketchos, Craypas, etc.)
> Colored chalk on wet paper
> White and colored chalk on black or colored paper
> Crayon on white and colored paper
> Tissue paper collages and felt tip pens
> Three-dimensional paper techniques on flat surface
> Paper sculpture forms
> Felt pens and water color
> Simple printing materials
> Cut paper and tempera paint
> Cutting out crayon figures and pasting on colored background
> Experimenting with new combinations of materials
> Decorating modeled forms of salt ceramic and papier maché with acrylic or tempera paints
> Gluing feathers, yarn, cotton, felt and other textural materials to modeled objects

Certain directed observations can help a child focus on a variety of aspects which might otherwise be overlooked.

Computing the Results

In order to gauge the effectiveness of a motivation and to determine the direction to follow in future motivations, it is desirable to have some means of evaluation. As children grow in responding to stimulation, teachers and parents can also grow in developing skills in guiding, inspiring, arousing, and instigating.

To check the content or structure, the Spirit and Strength Check List on page 20 can be utilized. Points to consider in maintaining the motivational dialogue on page 18 will also be useful. These factors should be reviewed frequently.

A motivation may be considered effective when a majority of the children have shown a highly personal involvement[23] with the subject matter presented. If a wide range of responses are given by the class, the motivation was broad and divergent in scope and was successful in encouraging uniqueness.

Investigate each item or part carefully for a full harvest of ideas.

How many sides to an idea?

How many aesthetic impressions make a visualized form?

What shape is an idea?

What color shall I give it?

Art is a response of the individual to a stimulus.

Art practice helps the child become more articulate in the use of art forms and helps him reach out for elusive ideas which are adrift or are not completely visualized.

In contrast to the character of accumulated knowledge, the essence of studio learning is intuitive, felt, and nonrational. In the making of a work of art, it is the compelling drive to bring into harmony and wholeness the insipient feeling or idea, material, and form. In the study of a work of art, it is the empathic discovery of fragments of meaning in the symbolism, form, and total configuration of the work that is the source of the aesthetic experience.

Manuel Barkan
from "Curriculum and the Teaching of Art"
REPORT OF THE COMMISSION ON ART EDUCATION
Jerome J. Hausman, editor
National Art Education Association
1201 16th St. NW, Washington, D.C. 20036, 1965

Fundamental Art Skills:
Aesthetic Qualities and Expressive Forms Developed

Aesthetic qualities and expressive forms are the principal fundamental art skills which can be computed from viewing the completed art product and from observing the child during the act of creating his work. The Teacher's Check List indicates points for the teacher to consider in measuring the child's involvement and growth in art.

Teacher's Check List
Does the child show an increase in ability to:

> Observe details and relate ideas with expression?
> Organize color, texture, line, shape, light and dark?
> Compare objects and things in terms of similarities and differences?
> Visualize familiar subject matter in a new way?
> Investigate divergent avenues?
> Select appropriate materials for the subject expressed?
> Seek additional information when it is needed?
> Experiment with a variety of materials?
> Remain engrossed in expressing his ideas?
> Become self-motivated in art following life's experiences?

Part of the computation also involves the child's analysis of his own art experience and product. The Child's Check List presents points for the child to consider.

Child's Check List

Did I make the figures large enough for this idea?

Did I use colors that gave my picture the right feeling?

Would I use the same colors the next time?

Would I select the same materials for this idea next time?

Did I need more information to tell about the subject and what it is doing?

Do I need to think more carefully about how I feel about the subject as well as how it looks?

Can I think of a way of drawing another picture about a similar topic?

Did I fill the page with my picture?

Would using light and dark colors tell my story better?

Did I use large and small textures in my picture?

Is the idea I wanted to show clear and easy to see?

Would this picture fit better on a tall paper, long paper, round paper, larger paper, smaller paper?

Did I enjoy making my picture?

Could I make the ground and sky more interesting in any way?

Did I show the necessary action for my topic?

Did I show enough details to express what I had in mind?

Did I draw any of the parts of my picture in a new or different way?

Could I do this picture over and draw it better?

Did I discover some of the limitations of the material I used?

Did I discover new ways to make textures, use colors, lines, and shapes?

Did I discover any new ways to use my material?

Briefly, it may be said that if a richer and more pleasing arrangement of the shapes, lines, and colors is arrived at than had previously been done, the child is growing aesthetically as a result of an inner integrative process. If the child shows significant deviations and changes from the manner in which he usually draws or models, if he exaggerates a particular part of the picture and adds a concentration of details, he has in all probability increased the fluency and flexibility of his thoughts and emotions. If more unique and imaginative ideas are presented than previously, the motivation has succeeded in arousing creative thinking.

As the desire to communicate visually increases, so grows the child's skill in handling the materials if motivations are presented frequently and regularly.

Start with a point of view and then expand it.

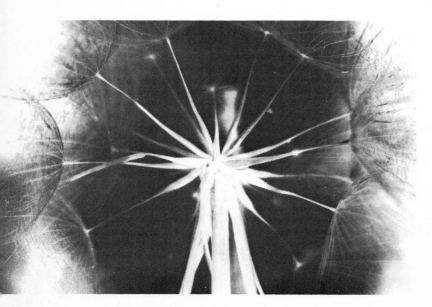

The value of the divergent question is that it requires the student to look at a content area from a variety of viewpoints and to participate in an imaginative way in answering the questions.

Robert Burkhart
from SPONTANEOUS AND DELIBERATE
WAYS OF LEARNING IN ART
Scranton: International Textbook Company
1962, p. 217

Divergent Paths for Next Time

Pursuit of art is an ongoing and unfolding experience which can be aided and extended through appropriate motivations.[24] Part or all of the written motivation may be used, and it can be profitably repeated at a later date. From it may grow an extension and expansion of ideas to be explored at a future time. All motivations and their "Divergent Paths" may need to be modified to be advantageous to the age of the children, the location of the school and home, and the background of the children's cultural experiences. In the quest for a stronger commitment and greater depth in children's aesthetic responses, Divergent Paths sections in Part II offer rich treasures for exploration and discovery.

Through the leads suggested under Divergent Paths, many types of motivations can be developed from those involving verbal interchange to those requiring acting-it-out, exploration of actual objects,[25] observation walks and rides, films, books, poems, records, photograph and slide collections, imagination stretchers, point-of-view changers, and cluster activities. The scope of divergent paths upon which a class will tread need only be limited by the creativity of the teacher. The responsibility is a major one as is the privilege of developing creativity and fluency of self-expression in the lives of children.

1. VIOLA, WILHELM, *Child Art*, 2nd ed., Peoria, Illinois: Chas. A. Bennett Co., Inc.

2. COLE, NATALIE, *The Arts in the Classroom*, New York: The John Day Company, Inc., Publishers, 1940.

3. LOWENFELD, VIKTOR, and BRITTAIN, W. LAMBERT, *Creative and Mental Growth*, 4th ed., New York: The Macmillan Company, 1964.

4. MENDELOWITZ, DANIEL C., *Children Art Artists*, Stanford, California: Stanford University Press, 1954.

5. KEILER, MANFRED, *Art in the Schoolroom*, Lincoln, Nebraska: University of Nebraska Press, 1955.

6. MATTIL, EDWARD L., *Meaning in Crafts*, 2nd ed., Englewood Cliffs, N. J., Prentice-Hall, Inc., 1965.

7. WANKELMAN, WILLARD and others, *Arts and Crafts for Elementary Teachers*, Dubuque, Iowa: Wm. C. Brown Company, Publishers, 1954.

8. JEFFERSON, BLANCHE, *Teaching Art to Children*, Boston: Allyn and Bacon, Inc., 1963.

9. McFEE, JUNE KING, *Preparation for Art*, Belmont, California: Wadsworth Publishing Co., 1960.

10. LINDERMAN, E. W., and HERBERHOLZ, DONALD W., *Developing Artistic and Perceptual Awareness*, Dubuque, Iowa: Wm. C. Brown Company Publishers, 1964.

11. CONRAD, GEORGE, *The Process of Art Education in the Elementary School*, Englewood Cliffs, N. J.: Prentice-Hall, Inc., 1964.

12. WACHOWIAK, FRANK, and RAMSAY, THEODORE, *Emphasis: Art*, Scranton, Pennsylvania: International Textbook Company, 1965.

13. GAITSKILL, CHARLES, *Children and Their Act*, New York: Harcourt, Brace and Company, 1958.

14. HERBERHOLZ, DONALD and BARBARA, "Base Line Deviations," *Schools Art*, Vol. 58, No. 2, pp. 33-35, Oct. 1958.

15. HEFFERNAN, HELEN, from an address presented to *American Childhood Educational International*, New York, April, 1965.

16. FOSHAY, ARTHUR, "The Creative Process Described," *Creativity in Teaching* ed. by Alice Miel, Belmont, California: Wadsworth Publishing Company, 1961.

17. HERBERHOLZ, BARBARA and DONALD, "The Way to the Creek," *Everyday Art*, Vol. 44, Fall, 1965. The American Crayon Co., Sandusky, Ohio.

18. KINCAIDA, CLARENCE, "The Determination and Description of Various Creative Attributes of Children," *Creativity and Art Education*, published by the National Art Education Association, Washington, D. C., 1964.

19. BRUNER, JEROME, *The Process of Education*, New York: Vintage Books, 1960.

20. HERBERHOLZ, BARBARA, "Christian Motivation," *School Arts*, Vol. 59, No. 3, Nov. 1959, p. 16.

21. HERBERHOLZ, DONALD, "Stimulation by Film," *School Arts*. Vol. 62, No. 4, pp. 25-26, 1962.

22. HERBERHOLZ, DONALD, "An Experimental Study to Determine the Effect of Modeling on the Drawing of the Human Figure by Second Grade Children," *National Art Education Association 9th Yearbook*, 1959, pp. 65-69.

23. McVITTY, LAWRENCE, "An Experimental Study of Various Methods in Art Motivation at the Fifth Grade Level," *National Art Education Association Yearbook*, 1956.

24. CLEMENTS, ROBERT, and others, "The Effectiveness of Three Motivational Methods in an Art Program in the Elementary Grades," U. S. Dept. of Health, Education, and Welfare, Project No. S-388, Feb., 1967.

25. ULMER, ROBERT P., "Perceptual Cues and Concept Enrichment in Children's Drawings." (Unpublished doctoral dissertation.) The Pennsylvania State University, 1966.

PART II:
Motivational Dialogues

Direct Happenings...Child in a Situation

This extensive group of motivations deals with recalling and rediscovering the direct personal experiences in which children participate in their daily lives. These situational occurrences can be discussed and elaborated upon with each child bringing forth ideas derived from the wellsprings of his personal primary experiences.

Questions favorable for contemplative pursuits stimulate thinking and provoke remembered feelings and sensations that cannot always be expressed in words but which will be relived and reorganized as the child draws, paints, cuts, or models. Since many of the answers to questions posed in the motivations deal with feelings, a verbal response should not always be expected. The colors used, the items portrayed, and the way in which they are depicted in the art expression will reveal what captured the child's imagination.

Reactivating inner and outer perceived stimuli in a motivation can trigger enlivened responses. The teacher's enthusiasm, excitement, and interest in the subject is contagious. As the child responds mentally, emotionally, physically, and perceptually, the motivation acts as a compass to help him navigate around and through his thoughts, feelings, and perceptions with a deepened concentration that ties these entities into a new wholeness resulting in a rich detailed involvement with the experience itself. The same topic may later be repeated or extended with the topics suggested under Divergent Paths since the child is constantly changing, forming, arranging, discovering, and building new relationships.

Verbal Interchange. . . . .The Magic of Remembering

Interchange — exchange, counterchange, transpose, swap, reciprocate, commute, give and take

Verbal interchange as a motivational technique involves an enlivened verbal interchange between the teacher and the children. New relationships and fresh inner feelings are generated, formed, and reformed as the discussion continues and the child becomes immersed in the topic. Sometimes a silent response is "thought" about by the child. This allows each child to form a different and unique yet "correct" answer or idea.

If the verbal interchange is considered a "group brain-storming session" and is enlivened with colorful questions, action-packed phrases, and provocative ideas, it will open new worlds of awareness and will help the child rediscover a particular happening or situation. When memory patterns are triggered, the child is free to unify and invent new conceptualized symbols for his art products.

THE EAST RIVER, Maurice Prendergast
Courtesy of: Collection, The Museum of Modern Art, New York
Gift of Abby Aldrich Rockefeller

Photo Credit: Sharon Corcoran

Verbal Interchange

WHAT I LIKE TO DO ON THE PLAYGROUND

We all like to play on the playground. We have some play equipment here at school, and perhaps you have visited parks and playgrounds where you could try out some other apparatus. What do you like to play best of all? Some boys and girls like to swing very high. How do you hold your hands when you swing? How do you hold your feet? Do you stand or sit on the swing? If you go high, does your stomach tickle? How do your feet help you pump yourself higher and higher? Does someone push you?

Some boys and girls like to climb and hang on the bars and on jungle gyms. Can you swing by your knees upside down? How does the world

look that way? Does it make the blood run to your head? Where are your arms when you hang by your knees? Do your knees get tired? What else can you do on the jungle gym? When a girl hangs by her knees, where does her hair fall?

How does it feel to hang by your arms from the high bars? How do you climb up to the top? What do you do with your hands? If you hold with your hands and drop, does it yank and jerk your armpits and make your feet tingle? Did you ever get dizzy looking down from the top? How do your arms begin to feel if you hang from a bar too long? What causes the bars to feel slippery sometimes? How do you feel if one of your friends pushes you and makes you fall? How many children are usually on the bars or jungle gym at one time? How many different things can you do on the gym? Did you ever pretend you were climbing a mountain or flying a plane when you are on the top?

How do you sit when you go down a slide? Where are your legs, knees, arms? Do you go fast? How do you land? Do you ever go down any other way than seated? How do you climb up the ladder? Where do your hands go? Did you ever fall off the ladder? Or did you land too hard when you slid down? When you were quite young, were you frightened when you first played on a slide? Did you ever go down any other kind of slide than a straight one? Some slides even land in a swimming pool for a big splash.

Did you ever swing across on the parallel rings? How many rings are there? How do you start across? How large are the rings and where do you hold them? Does it make your arms tired to swing across? Where do you feel the pull the most? Where are your feet and what are they doing as you swing across? Do you look up or down as you go? Do you find yourself short of breath?

Who likes the teeter totter the best? How do you sit on it? Do you play on it alone? How is the teeter totter shaped? How do you use your feet and where do you hold your hands? Do you like to go up high? Did you ever bounce hard when your end of the board went down fast?

What other play equipment have you played on? Can you tell us about it?

Draw a picture about what you like to do on the playground.

Verbal Interchange
PICKING FRUIT

What is your favorite fruit? Cherries, peaches, apples, apricots, pears? Did you ever pick any fruit right off the tree and eat it? Was it warm and sweet from the sun? Could you reach it from the ground? How high was the branch? Taller than you? Did you stand on tiptoe and still find you couldn't reach the fruit? What did you do then? Perhaps you climbed the tree or found a ladder. Were the branches heavy and thick and bent over from the weight of the fruit? Were there a lot of leaves on the tree? Was the bark rough? What color was the fruit? Was it soft or firm? Did you put the fruit in a bucket or sack or basket? Was anyone helping you? How were you dressed? Was it a hot day? How much fruit did you pick before you climbed down from the tree or from the ladder?

Draw a picture about a time when you picked fruit from a large tree. Make the tree as tall as the paper. Show yourself picking the fruit.

Backyard fun calls for plenty of war whoops plus head bands, feathers, loin cloths.

Dancing around the campfire is always part of pretending to be Indians.

What sort of dance are these young braves *doing*?

Verbal Interchange

WE ARE PLAYING INDIAN

Under each picture is a verbal comment which can be coordinated with the accompanying picture. Use of the opaque projector is recommended.

After showing the pictures, the teacher can ask if the children themselves have played Indian. Questions that could be used might include some concerning how the children dress while playing and what they did. They will then be asked to express their ideas about it visually. The teacher may wish to collect additional pictures of some real Indians to show to the children during the discussion.

Buffalo or paleface better watch out.

And after a hard day's hunt, a good meal of rabbit and corn around the campfire. Squaw and pappoose wait at the teepee.

Indians live in different types of homes. This one is made of wood.

Verbal Interchange

MY BIRTHDAY PARTY

Everyone likes to go to a birthday party. What are some of the things you did at your last birthday party? What happened after you greeted your guests at the door? Did you play games? What kind? How many presents did you receive? Were they wrapped with bright paper and tied with lots of pretty colored ribbon? Did you wear perky party hats? What kind of cake did you have? Was it decorated? How? Or did you have cupcakes? What else did you have to eat and drink? Did you sit around a table? Did you blow out all the candles at once? How did you feel when your friends sang "Happy Birthday to You"?

Not all birthday parties are held at home. "King" Eric's party was held in a "castle" complete with a throne, crown, and a dragon puppet that told funny stories.

Make a picture about your birthday party.

Verbal Interchange
WE ARE SINGING CHRISTMAS CAROLS

Here in America and in many countries, singing Christmas carols is enjoyed by boys and girls. Will any of you be going out and singing Christmas carols this year? It is usually done at night by a small group of children. Where do you go to sing? Who would hear you? How would you dress? Who would be with you? What would the weather be like? What would you see around you? How will you feel inside? When you are singing, how do you hold the songbook? How will you hold your mouth when you are singing? Do you suppose it will be cold enough to see your breath?

Draw, paint, or cut and paste a picture about yourself and your friends singing Christmas carols.

Verbal Interchange

MY FRIENDS AND I ARE CLIMBING
A MOUNTAIN

We live close to some very high mountains. What are their names? Have you ever climbed a mountain? Was it steep? Did you go up a trail? What was the trail like? Was it straight like a sidewalk or curving like a ribbon? Did you find a strong walking stick to use? What were you carrying? Did you have a canteen? Did you wear a cap or hat to protect you from the hot sun? Do you know what a knapsack is? Many hikers carry their equipment in one on their backs. Do you suppose you would need good heavy boots if the trail were rocky? What if the trail stopped and heavy craggy rocks and cliffs kept you from the top of the peak? Did you ever see real professional mountain climbers use ropes to tie themselves to each other so if one fell, his friend could catch him? How do you suppose it would feel to look down for hundreds of feet and see jagged rocks below you? Some mountain climbers have even come upon an eagle's nest high up in the rocks. You might see mountain cabins as you climbed and, of course, you would probably see quite a few trees. What would you find at the top of the mountain?

Draw yourself and your friends climbing a high, rugged mountain.

Verbal Interchange
WE ARE CLIMBING TREES

Who has climbed a tree? How large was it? Was the trunk as big around as you are? Can you remember the branches and which ones you grabbed and pulled yourself up on? Were there any low branches? Any broken ones? Was the bark rough and scratchy? Did you tear your clothes? Was there a place to sit in the tree? Was there a tree house in it? Did you see any knotholes, birds' nests, blossoms, fruit, buds, twigs, leaves, squirrels? Did any branches bend when you sat on them? How high up did you go? Did anyone climb the tree with you? What were you wearing? How did you get down?

Can you make a picture about you climbing a tree?

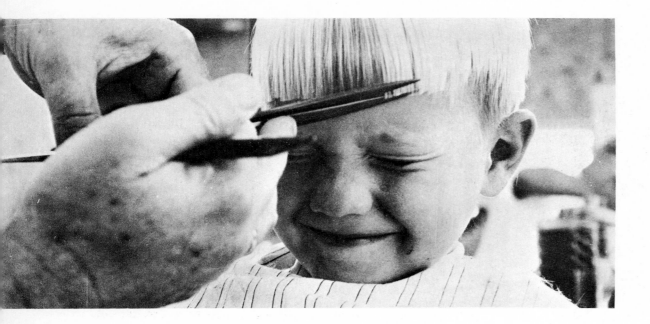

Verbal Interchange
I GET A HAIR CUT

Do you remember where you sit when you get a haircut? How high up was the seat? Where did you put your feet? What did the barber put around you to keep your clothes clean? How was the barber dressed? Did he stand or sit? What could you see in front of you while you sat there? Where was the mirror? What colors and shapes were the bottles of lotions and hair oil? What tools did the barber use? Did any of them make noises? Did he use a scissors? Where did your hair fall when it was cut? How did the brush feel on your neck? Did any short hair fall inside your shirt and feel scratchy? Did the hair oil smell good? Did you enjoy having your hair cut? Did you cry the first time you went or can you remember so long ago? How did you feel when you left the shop?

Make a picture about having your hair cut.

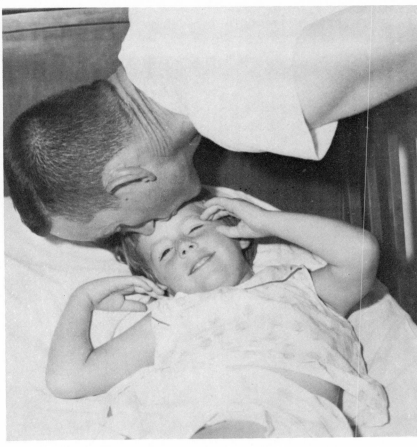

Photo Credit: Sharon Corcoran

Photo Credit: Sharon Corcoran

Verbal Interchange

I Am Sleeping

Think for a few minutes of being very tired and sleepy and how good it feels to go to sleep. All of us need rest and sleep every night and, after a long day of playing, studying, or working, most of us are glad to stretch out or curl up in bed and sleep. Do you prefer to sleep in a dark room or do you like a night light burning? Do you prefer a warm room or do you like to open a window and have a lot of fresh air? All of us like the fresh clean smell of sheets that have dried out in the sun and wind. Some people toss around a lot before they go to sleep, and some fall asleep the minute their heads touch the pillow. What kind of sleeper are you? In what position do you sleep? Some people curl up in a cozy ball and some stretch out. Some put their knees up, some sleep on their stomachs.

Model yourself sleeping. Make it in any position you like. Think of where your knees are, elbows, and head. Where does your back bend? Are your feet crossed?

TEACHER'S NOTE:

This material is especially suitable for use with modeling any material such as plasticene clay, the regular hardening clay, or salt ceramic material.

Photo Credit: Jon Else

Verbal Interchange
I Am Feeding the Ducks and Geese

Did you ever feed ducks and geese? How did you do it? Show us. Did you throw seed or bird food or bread crumbs to them? Was the food in a bag or a box? How did you throw it? Did you throw it far? Birds get hungry in the cold days of winter and enjoy the food you give them. Did they stand on the ground and peck at it? Or did they grab it from your hand? Did they dip their heads in water? Did the feed fall through your fingers? Were there more birds up in the sky or in the bushes watching? How do you suppose it feels to eat like birds eat, without hands or forks and spoons? Did you sit or stand to feed them? Was anyone with you? Were the birds colorful? Did you talk to the birds? Did they chirp, peep, or chatter?

Paint a picture about when you fed the ducks and geese. Remember to use large brushes for the larger things in the picture, and small brushes for details. Let the underneath color dry before painting on top of it.

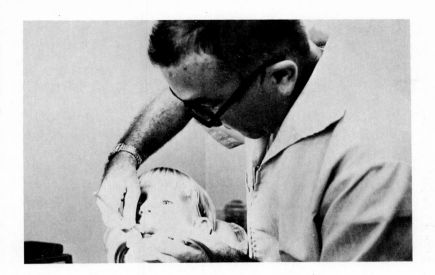

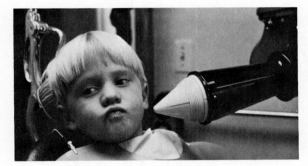

Verbal Interchange
WHEN I WENT TO THE DENTIST

When did you last visit your dentist? Where is his office? What is his office like? Did you look at magazines in the waiting room? Who went with you? Were you excited? Or were you a little afraid? One dentist has a treasure chest into which the children may look and choose a surprise before they leave. His patients are usually too busy thinking about what gift they will select to be nervous.

Was there a nurse in the office? How was she dressed? What was the chair like that you sat in when the dentist looked at your teeth? Did you have to step up to get in it? Did the dentist stand or sit when he was working? How was he dressed? Where did he keep his tools and instruments? Did the nurse clip a bib around your neck? What instruments did you see? Did your dentist take an X-ray? How did the X-ray plate feel in your mouth? Did the spotlight bother your eyes? What shape was the tall machine beside the chair? How large was the round tray in front of you? What was on the tray?

How did it feel to keep your mouth open wide for a long time? Did you experience any new tastes? How did the drill feel? What material did he use to fill your tooth? Did the dentist's hands feel large? Did you ever have a tooth pulled? How did it feel? Did it bleed? Did he need to use a local anesthetic? What instrument did he use? Did he let you keep the tooth he pulled?

Draw a picture about your visit to the dentist.

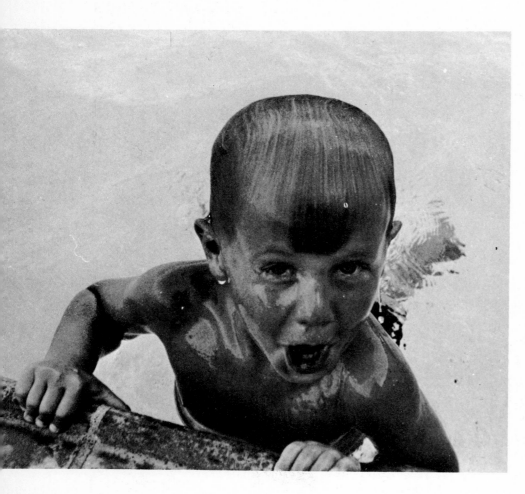

Verbal Interchange
WE ARE SWIMMING

It will soon be the "good old summertime" and that means boys and girls will be swimming again. Where do you plan to go swimming? Will it be at the beach or in a pool or in a river? What does the water look like? Is it cool? What color is it?

How do you get into the water? Do you first put in one toe to see how cold the water is? Or are you brave and just jump in feet first or maybe even head first? How does it feel when you first hit the water and get all wet? Do you shiver and see goose bumps on your legs? How does it feel when you open your eyes under water? Does it hurt? What can you see? Do you feel heavy or light in the water? Is it easy to walk fast in waist deep water? How do your arms and legs move when you swim? Do you keep your head under the water or out of the water when you swim? How does it feel to float on a tube in the water and let the sun shine down on your face? Can anyone dive? How does it feel to dive off the diving board into the water? How does your head feel when it hits the water? Do you hold your breath and close your eyes? How do you feel when you get out of the water? Does your suit feel heavy and wet and cold? Do your ears get filled with water? Do you wear a cap? Do you brush the hair out of your eyes? Do you wrap yourself in a towel to get dry? Do you lie on the cement around the pool to get warm?

Make a picture about yourself and your friends swimming. Cut and tear poster paper and tissue paper and then paste. Don't draw it first. Make yourself out of the poster paper using different colors for the different parts. Use the tissue for the "water." Secure the whole picture to a 12" x 18" or larger white paper background.

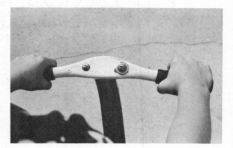

Verbal Interchange

I AM RIDING MY SCOOTER

How fast can you go on your scooter? When you are going very, very fast, is it hard to balance it? Do you place both feet on the scooter? How do you make it go fast again when it starts to slow down? Which foot do you keep on the scooter? Do you lean forward when you go fast? Where do you put your hands? How do you turn a corner? How do you make it stop? Did you ever squat down while your scooter was going downhill and just coast? Did you ever hit a bump and fall off? Are you taller than your scooter? Do you like to go fast or just coast along? What color is your scooter?

Draw yourself riding your scooter.

Verbal Interchange
I Am Fishing

When you go fishing, do you go to the ocean, a river, a lake, or a pond in the park? Do you go by yourself or does some friend or your father go with you? Do you take your bike, the family car, or do you walk? What clothes do you wear? Do you go fishing in the summer or in the winter or both? Do you go early in the morning or at noon or in the evening before the sun goes down? How do you dress to go fishing? Do you have your own fish line and pole? Do you dig bait or buy the bait you use? Do you take extra hooks and something to carry the fish in which you hope to catch? Before you throw your line in the water, do you put the bait on and decide on the proper hook? Do you use a sinker? Do you use a float? Do you cast the line out or let the water current carry it out to the fish? How can you tell when you have a fish on the line? Can you tell if it is a big or small one? Do some fish fight more after they have been hooked than others? Have you ever caught such a big fish that someone else had to help you turn your reel to land it? How does the fish feel when you take him off the hook? Is he slippery? Did you ever have a fish stick its fins into your hand when you took it off the hook? How do you like the smell of fish? Do you clean your own fish or does father or big brother help you? Are you sometimes disappointed when you don't catch any fish?

Draw a picture about going fishing.

___

Teacher's Note:
A short piece of string can be glued to the picture by the child to serve as a fishline.

Photo 1.

Photo 3.

Photo 2.

Photos 4 and 4a.

PRODUCE

Photo 5.

Photo 6.

Photo 8.

Photo 9.

Photo 10.

Verbal Interchange

The accompanying photographs can be shown during the verbal interchange. An opaque projector is recommended for showing the photos which will aid in recall of the experience.

AT THE SUPER MARKET

Photo 1.   Heidi sits in the cart at the super market. Who pushes the cart when you go shopping?

Photo 2.   Rows and racks of bread line the long shelves. How many shapes of loaves do you see? What colors are the wrappings and labels? Can you reach the top shelf? The super market, and especially the bread aisle, is a busy place.

Photo 3.   Robert's sister helps him select some cookies from the many varieties, and they put the packages in the cart. How many wheels are on the cart? It is a rectangular basket made of wire. Are you as tall as the handle or are you taller?

Photos 4 and *4a.*   Daddy weighs bananas on the hanging scale. What other produce do you find in the market? What colors and shapes are they? Are they piled in neat stacks or rows? Are some in little baskets or bags?

Photo 5.   Would you choose licorice, chocolate, mint wafers, tangerine slices, or chicken bones from these glistening bags?

Photo 6.   Joey and Helen found bright colored spirals of lollipops on a merry-go-round rack.

Photo 7.   Hamburger, steaks, pork chops, pot roasts, liver, chicken. The butcher has arranged the packages in the refrigerated bin.

Photo 8.   Tall cans, short cans, bottles, and jars. Which will your mother choose?

Photo 9.   Peggy hugs her teddy bear as the cart rolls up to the cashier.

Photo 10.   The cashier at the cash register rings up the cost of each individual item and adds the total on a long strip of paper. How does the cashier dress? Can you see the rows of numbers he presses and the reel of trading stamps?

Draw a picture about shopping at the super market.

MANCHESTER VALLEY, Joseph Pickett
Courtesy of: Collection, The Museum of Modern Art, New York
Gift of Abby. Aldrich Rockefeller

On Location . . . Walks and Rides

Location — place, situation, locale, site, position, post, neighborhood, environment, spot

Both walking and riding trips allow children to experience at first hand a direct happening "on location." Walking to an adjacent or nearby spot makes possible a number of excursions. More distant places require transportation, and arrangements should be carefully made in advance to avoid disappointments and mishaps.

Groundwork before the trip is important. A frame of reference supports the child in the pursuit of such discoveries as:

What the shapes and functions of things are
What the textures are
What odors will be encountered
What colors he might look for
What noises he might hear
How these findings are related to those things which he already knows

When the children return from a location, a short discussion can direct them in investigating the personalized concepts, percepts, and ideas that they have derived from the freshly experienced direct happening.

On Location

WE VISIT THE ZOO

Before the visit: When we visit the zoo, some things to look for are the tallest animal, the longest animal, the fattest, and the one that is the brightest color. Try to see all the different kinds of cages and homes the animals and birds and reptiles have. What do you suppose they will be eating? Will some be sleeping or playing? What different kinds of noises and sounds will you hear? Remember to listen carefully. See which ones have babies. Which ones like peanuts? Find the animal with the longest toenails.

Upon return: (Reexamine above questions and sum up with the following:) Which animal would you like to ride? How about a dippy ride on the hippo while he is in the muddy water? How do you suppose it would feel to roar like a lion? Perhaps that's why he has small ears! Did you ever try to run like an antelope? Which animal had a pattern on his coat of fur? Which animal had the largest mouth? The longest legs? The longest neck? Weighed the most? Was the brightest color? Was the best swimmer? Had horns? Could talk? Sang the best? Could swing by his tail? Was the most frightening? If you could be any animal in the zoo for one day, which would you be? Draw that one.

TEACHER'S NOTE:

In addition to painting, drawing, cutting, and pasting, this particular motivation is well suited to any of the modeling or three-dimensional materials. A cluster activity would be an excellent terminating and culminating project.

FIGURE OF A HIPPOPOTAMUS, From Tomb of Senbi, at Meir
Courtesy of: The Metropolitan Museum of Art
Gift of Edward S. Harkness, 1917

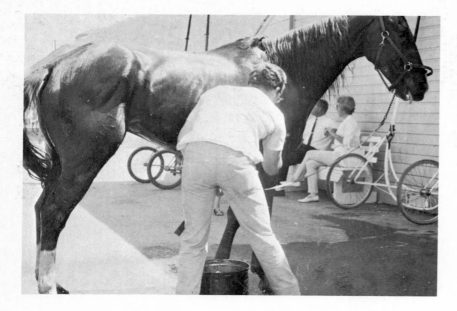

On Location

These pages could be shown to the class on the opaque projector before going to a horse show, or, if such a trip is impossible to arrange, the vicarious experience involved in viewing the photographs will serve in lieu of the actual experience. If children have attended a horse show, a closer re-examination of details in the photographs will jog and reactivate memories.

AT THE HORSE SHOW

The magnificent horses are perfectly groomed before the competition begins. How is a show horse's mane different from a cowboy's horse?

The men and women wear a special clothing called a riding habit. What color is it? Why do they wear numbers on their backs? What sort of boots do the riders wear? How many different shapes of hats did you see?

A show horse must be a very proud creature. He must stand tall and show good form as well as a good performance. He must obey his rider, too.

How is a bridle worn by the horse? What kind of saddle do these riders use? What are the spurs for? How are some horses' hoofs different from those of other horses?

Judges watch carefully as the horses take the hurdles. Horse and rider must work together and show their best performance. Does the rider lean forward as the horse starts the jump? How many different kinds of hurdles did you see? Did any of the horses knock down the hurdles? How do you suppose the rider felt when that happened?

What were the prizes that were given? How would you feel if you won a prize?

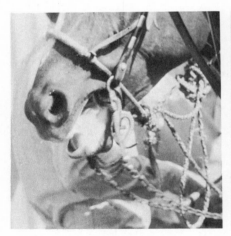

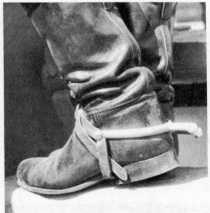

SUGGESTED TOPICS:

    My horse at the horse show
    Grooming a horse for the horse show
    Riding a horse in a fox hunt
    Jumping a hurdle at the horse show

Photo 1.

Photo 2.

On Location

If a trip to a Farmer's Market is possible, the accompanying pictures could be shown with an opaque projector prior to the trip to indicate the things to look for during the visit. If such a trip is not possible, showing of the pictures to the children will serve in lieu of the actual experience.

Photo 3.

Photo 4.

Photo 5.

Photo 6.

Photo 7.

WE VISIT THE FARMER'S MARKET

Photo 1. Farmers bring crates of freshly picked vegetables and fruit to the market place on trucks. They open the wooden crates and unpack ears of corn, cantaloupe, peaches, tomatoes, or whatever may be the season's harvest. Each farmer and his family has a booth in which to sell the produce.

Photo 2. The farmer's children ride along on the truck to help their father unload and sort out the round, ripe tomatoes to be weighed and sold to early morning shoppers. Do you suppose they like to ride in their father's truck?

Photo 3. Grandmother helps arrange juicy, sweet peaches in neat rows in the family booth. She wears a clean apron and enjoys helping customers make their selections.

Photo 4. Farmers weigh some vegetables before they price them for sale. Other vegetables are packed in little cartons or trays. What vegetables did you see in Farmer's Market? Which vegetables were red? Which were orange? Which were yellow? Which were green? Who saw a purple vegetable?

Photo 5. These summer, crookneck, and zucchini squash have different textures and shapes.

Photo 6. How many colors of beans did you see? This little girl is helping her mother select some yellow wax beans from a huge pile.

Photo 7. Did you ever see so many cucumbers? These will be made into pickles. What color are cucumbers? Are they rough or smooth? What do they look like inside?

Photo 8. Craig wanted his mother to buy some crisp carrots. After looking at several of the farmers' booths, he and his mother decided to make their purchases.

Photo 9. A crate of plump green peppers waits in the sun for a prospective buyer. These are green but some peppers are bright red. Do you like peppers?

Photo 10. Money is paid to the farmer's wife as a shopper buys a dozen ears of corn. The farmer's wife will put the corn in a paper bag and the customer will carry it home to cook and eat. Is corn your favorite vegetable?

Photo 8.

Photo 9.

Photo 10.

SUGGESTED TOPICS FOR DRAWING, PAINTING AND MODELING

Helping father unload the vegetables
Arranging the fruit and vegetables in the booth
Helping mother select vegetables for dinner
Buying fruits or vegetables
Helping mother carry vegetables home

On Location

RIDING A STEAM LOCOMOTIVE

A sharp blast of the whistle, and we'll be off for a real ride on an old-fashioned steam locomotive! Why do you suppose this type of train was called an "iron horse"? First, we must buy our tickets and then we'll board the coach or open-air excursion car or maybe the caboose for a ride on the narrow-gauge rails.

The conductor punched our tickets. **How was he** dressed? What was on his head? As the train clacked across the yard switches and around the yard-throat bend, what did you see? What was that old wooden water tank used for? After the engine had quenched its thirst, we rounded a hairpin curve and gently descended into the pear orchards. Could you feel the vibrations, smell the smoke spewing out, see the steam pouring from every pore of the engine as we entered the woods and started up the grade?

How was the engineer dressed?

Did you see the engineer checking the locomotive when we stopped? His oil can was three feet high! What did he do with it? How was the engine shaped? How did the wheels work? Did you see the old lantern on the end of the caboose? How did the engine look from the front? From the side?

What was on top of the engine?

Where will you place the engine on the page? Will you show some track? How large was the engine? Was it taller than the engineer? How long was the whole train? How many cars were there?

SUGGESTED TOPICS FOR DRAWING, PAINTING AND MODELING

    Engineer oiling the train
    Engineer driving the train
    We are going up a steep grade
    Conductor taking our tickets

Giving the locomotive a drink from the old wooden tank
Steam locomotive coming into the station
Getting on the locomotive

    NOTE — Steam locomotive pictured here is the Camino, Cable, and Northern RR. operating at Camino, California.

On Location

AT THE SERVICE STATION

Before the trip: We are going to walk over to the corner service station this morning. Look for things you never noticed before and re-look at some of the things you are accustomed to seeing at a service station. What sounds do you think you will hear, and what odors will you smell? When we have spent about ten minutes there, we will return to class and draw what each of us thought was the most interesting thing about our trip. All of you have been in service stations before when your family drove in to have gas put in the car. Would you like to work in a gas station? Why or why not? What does the attendant do? How does he fill the gas tanks of the cars? How does he check the oil? Where is the cash register? What does he do to your windshield? To your tires? Is he a busy man? What does he wear? How tall is he? How tall do you think the gas pumps are and what shape are they? What else will you see and hear and smell?

Upon return: Where did the cars enter the station? Could several cars be serviced at once? Was there a garage? How does the man lubricate the car and change the oil? Did you see a car raised up on a rack? Where were the rest rooms? Was a mechanic working? What did he do? What sounds did you hear? What odors did you smell? Do you like the smell of gasoline? Did you notice any stacks of oil cans or new tires? Show me how the attendant filled the car and checked the tires and washed the windshield. Did you notice his uniform? How was the building shaped? How many doors and windows? What color was it? How many gas pumps were there and where were they located? Which part of our trip was the most interesting to you?

Grade 1: Draw the attendant putting gas in your car.

Grade 2: Draw what you would do if you worked at a service station.

Grade 3: Draw the most interesting thing you remember about the service station.

Acting-It-Out . . . Seeing and Doing

Acting — performing, doing, functioning, exercising, committing, advancing, accomplishing, pretending, executing, operating, moving, motioning

In addition to verbal involvement, the actual physical re-enactment of a past experience will refresh the children's memory traces and help them to retrieve kinesthetic sensations. The acting-it-out technique provides a warm-up period in which the children are able to *feel* as well as to *see* which bodily parts are moved in the action being discussed. This is accomplished in two ways: First, one or two children go through the motions while the class watches so that they might see which bodily parts are moved in the performance, and, second, the entire class acts out the movements thus enabling each child to remember how it feels kinesthetically and to identify what his own muscles are doing.

Verbal interchange sets the stage for the integration of the child's thoughts, feelings, and perceptions that accompany acting-it-out. Such a line of questioning includes:

Where the action took place
How the participants were dressed
What the weather was like
When the action occurred
Who else was involved
How the children felt
What the size relationships, colors, weights, textures, and shapes were

Following the verbal interchange, the children will begin their artistic self-expression with the materials specified. An occasional word of encouragement or a reminder of some detail may be necessary to maintain the motivation of some of the children.

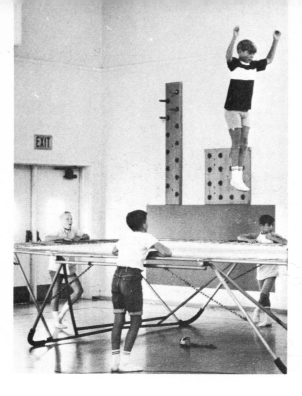

Acting-It-Out

Due to the plastic qualities of clay, it is recommended that it be used for this motivation. Children can manipulate the figure during the working process and make it go through the discussed motions.

I Am Taking Exercises

Who has taken exercises? Why do we take exercises? How do you do it? Who would like to show us one exercise? Watch his arms, his legs. Where does he bend his knees? How do his arms go? Let's all do that exercise now. Can you feel your leg muscles pulling or straining? Are you reaching high, high with your arms? Where does your head go? Who can show us a bending-in-the-middle exercise, a reaching or stretching exercise, push-ups, an exercise in which your body must twist? How does it feel to do it? Do you get out of breath? Can you feel your heart pound?

Watch and see where your elbows and hips bend. How does your head feel when you touch your toes? Do the backs of your knees hurt when you bend over and touch your toes?

Model yourself doing one of the exercises we have just demonstrated. The legs of your figure will have to be strong enough to stand on if you make a standing exercise. Try to make your figure doing something different from that of your neighbor.

Acting-It-Out
We Jump Rope Together

Jumping rope is a game that we are able to do alone or with friends. Jumping rope has been a favorite of children for many years. People once believed that the higher they could jump rope, the higher their crops would grow, and every spring they had a jumping contest. Now we usually singsong a rhyme as we jump that may tell a fortune such as how many children we'll have or how many spankings we'll get or what kind of job our future husband will have. Some jingles tell a story. What jingles do you say when you jump rope? Do you know what "peppers" or "hot" mean? (turn rope rapidly) What other special words do you know that describe things you do in jumping rope? Who can show us how to jump rope alone by turning the rope over your head? Can you jump forward and backward? Can you jump on one foot? How many times have you jumped without missing? Did you ever cross your arms while you were jumping?

(While child is demonstrating. . .)   Where are her arms when the rope goes up? When it goes down? How does she hold the handles? Does she bend her knees? Does she jump high? Does she jump on one foot or two? Is she running out of breath? Watch her pigtails bounce! Let's say a jingle with her and feel the rhythm.

Jumping rope can be done with your friends, too, with one holding each end of the rope and one or more children jumping in the middle. Who will show us how it is done? (While children are demonstrating. . .) Are they swinging the rope with one of their arms or both? See how high their arms must go to make the rope go all around. How do they place their feet? Can you run into the rope while it is turning and begin jumping? Can you run out while it is turning? Where

do the children who are jumping put their hands? Do they bend their knees or jump straight up and down? Do they jump on one foot or two? Sometimes the rope is turned back and forth in an arc and isn't turned all the way over the head of the jumper. One game calls for a long line of children, perhaps five or six, to line up and run through the rope one at a time without missing.

Draw a picture about jumping rope. (You may want to give each child a piece of string or yarn to paste on his paper for his "rope.")

—————

TEACHER'S NOTE:

RIMBLES, a book of children's Classic Games, Rhymes, Songs and Sayings by Patricia Evans, Doubleday & Co., Inc., Garden City, New York. For a marvelous collection of jump rope rhymes that have been handed down for generations, familiar and real memory-joggers as well as a host of new ones that set one's feet jumping almost automatically, this book is suggested. The teacher can read some to the class and can tell them about some jump rope games for several days before the motivation.

Acting-It-Out
I Am Pulling a Wagonload of Friends

Who has played with a wagon? What are some of the things you can do with a wagon besides pull it? What could you do with it upside down? What other object could you use with it to have fun? What color is your wagon? How large is it? What is the shape of a wagon? Where are the wheels? Where is the tongue? Did you ever pull a heavy load in a wagon? What was it? Was the ground bumpy or smooth? How does it feel to pull a wagonload up a hill? Is it different from going down a hill? How different? How do you pull a wagon? Show us. Where is your arm that is not pulling on the handle? How do you place your feet? Do you have to lean over somewhat? Did you ever pull your friends, or your brother or sister in a wagon? Where? Did your wagon wheels squeak? How many people are the most you ever pulled in a wagon? How did they sit? Where were their legs — in or out of the wagon? Did they face the front or side? Did you get tired? Let's choose several boys and girls to come up in front of the class and pretend they are pulling a wagonload of children. They will have to be strong and pull very hard.

Draw a picture about pulling a wagonload of friends.

Acting-It-Out

WE HAVE A TEA PARTY FOR OUR DOLLS

Did you ever wear dress-up clothes and high heels and big floppy hats and have a tea party for your dolls? You would need to use your very best doll dishes and set your tea table very carefully. Would you have a bouquet of flowers? Where would your dolls sit? Would you invite a few of your friends, too? Some friends might bring doll carriages and very fancy umbrellas and pretend to be very grown-up. What would you serve? How do you pour a cup of tea?

Can you draw a picture about having a tea party for your dolls?

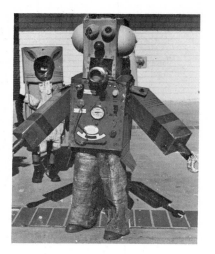

Acting-It-Out

Scaring Someone with My Halloween Costume

How will you dress this Halloween? Who will be something scary? Who will be in a funny costume? What colors are in your costume? Where will you go to scare someone? Do you like to go trick-or-treating? Will you wear a mask? Or will you wear makeup? What will you look like? What will you wear on your feet? On your head? What will you carry in your hands? Will you be excited? What if someone scares *you* instead? How will you scare people? Will you have a noisemaker? Will you use your arms? Can you describe your costume, part by part and from top to bottom? Does it have long sleeves; a belt; a tail; ears; a beard; parts; a full skirt; tights; a hat?

Make a picture about scaring someone when you are wearing your Halloween costume.

Teacher's Note:

The record, "Danse Macabre," can be played after which the teacher might ask children to pretend to scare someone on Halloween night.

Acting-It-Out

I Am Brushing My Teeth

When do you brush your teeth? Where? How? Who can show us? How do you apply the toothpaste to the brush? Could you brush without bending your elbow? Can you brush with your mouth closed? Do you stand or sit? How high is the bathroom sink? Do you brush your teeth up and down or sideways? How does the toothpaste taste? Do you bend over to spit and rinse? Where are the faucets? Does anyone use an electric toothbrush? Do your teeth feel clean when you are finished? Where do you put your brush when you are through? Is there a medicine cabinet above the sink and a towel rack beside the sink? How are you dressed when you brush?

Make a picture showing yourself brushing your teeth.

Acting-It-Out

PLAYING TAG

Do all of you know how to play tag? Children everywhere seem to enjoy the excitement of chasing and running. Where do you play tag? Do you do it often? Would you rather chase or be chased? Can you run very, very fast? Can you catch anyone you chase? How is running different from walking? Do you get out of breath when you run a lot? Do you get hot and sweaty in the summer? Did you ever watch your shadow when you run and try to run faster than it does? (The teacher can choose one of the children to run across the room.)

How were his legs when he ran? Could he run with both feet touching the floor at the same time? How high up did his knees go? What did he do with his arms? If you are chasing someone and are very close, how do you reach out and touch him? What if he stays just a few inches away, do you keep your arm out and keep trying to tag him as you run? Do you lean forward a little to go faster? What clothes do you wear when you are playing tag? Which are your best "running shoes"?

Draw a picture about playing tag.

Photo Credit: Jon Else

PRACTICE, Iver Rose
Courtesy of: E. B. Crocker Art Gallery
Sacramento, California

On the Spot . . . Actual Objects . . .
Actual — real, veritable, true, genuine, authentic, concrete, factual, existing, certain, touchable, tangible

Many motivations can be strengthened and vitalized by bringing an actual object into the classroom to use as a stimulator, activator, and interest-generator. Children are able to see visually the details, and to relate size, shape, texture, color, and action to the activity under discussion.

Real objects often act as links in a memory chain. The leathery smell and smooth hard surface of a saddle recalls for many children an exciting ride on a horse. The crunch of a juicy apple makes the child more aware of his teeth and mouth and will aid in recall of the smooth, red, shiny exterior and crisp, white interior of the apple.

Most of the objects handled in this type of motivation will be familiar to the children. The importance of the objects lies in their capacity to stir the children's memories, to sharpen their sensory capacities, and to trigger the creation of an aesthetic product.

On the Spot . . . Actual Object . . .
Various Musical Instruments

I Am Playing a Musical Instrument

Guitars, banjos, and autoharps are strummed, drums are beaten, horns and flutes are blown, accordions are squeezed, and pianos are played with the fingers. What other instruments do you know about? Which instrument do you play or would you like to play? Perhaps your older brother or sister plays a musical instrument. Which are made of wood? Which are metal? Which are larger than the player? Which are held in the hand? Do you think it takes a lot of blowing to make pleasant sounds? Can you show us how you hold a guitar (drum, flute, horn, violin, or some other instrument)?

Perhaps some of you have taken lessons or watched a band or an orchestra or quartet perform on the stage or on television. Where are the hands placed when using a certain instrument? Are the elbows bent? Are the arms lifted above the head? Would you sit or stand when you played it? How does the music sound? Is it usually loud or soft? How is the music of a violin different from a drum? Do you like fast or slow music? What would you wear if you were playing an instrument on a stage?

Make a picture about you or some group playing musical instruments.

Courtesy of: Olin Mathieson Chemical Corporation

Courtesy of: Conn . . . World's Largest Manufacturer of Band Instruments

HANDBALL, Ben. Shahn
Courtesy of: Collection, The Museum of Modern Art, New York
Abby Aldrich Rockefeller Fund

On the Spot . . . Actual Object . . . Large Ball

PLAYING CATCH WITH MY FRIEND

Which two children would like to demonstrate how to play catch? Stand about ten feet apart (closer for younger children). How do you throw the ball? Watch carefully. Did he use both hands? Did both of his arms reach way, way out far? Do you suppose he had to give it a good push so that it would reach his friend? How did his friend catch it? Were both of his arms stretched out very far? Did he catch it with a hand on each side of the ball? Does it ever drop through your hands and bounce away? If a friend throws the ball too hard, does it hurt your hands or hit you in the stomach or face? Do you ever bounce the ball back and forth to each other? If your friend throws it too high, do you have to jump up high off the ground to catch it? Or maybe you have to bend over and grab it if it is too low. Is it easier to catch a large ball or a small ball? What color of ball do you like best?

Draw yourself and your friend playing catch with a large ball. Think carefully which way you will draw this picture on the paper. How far apart will you put yourself and your friend? How tall will you make yourself on the paper?

Courtesy of: Japan Air Lines

Courtesy of: Japan Air Lines

On the Spot . . . Actual Object . . . Kite
I Am Flying My Kite

No one knows who invented kites, but it was someone a long time ago. A flat kite was used in China more than 2,000 years ago. Grown-ups and children in China, Japan, and Korea love kites and decorate them gaily. In China, the ninth day of the ninth month is Kites' Day. Kites have proved to be useful, too. Armies used to send signals with kites, and huge suspension bridges have been started with lines lifted across a canyon with kites. Weather instruments are carried aloft with kites. And long ago, an American called Benjamin Franklin used a kite to learn about electricity. Plain flat kites must have tails to keep them from taking a nose dive. Box kites don't have tails. Chinese kites often are in the shape of animals, fish, or insects. We need a gentle breeze, not a strong wind, to fly a kite.

Who can show us how to hold this kite to help get it aloft? Do you need a friend or your father to run with it or hold the string while you run? How do you hold the string, and where do you look when the kite finally gets airborne? Do your arms get tired holding the string? Does the kite dip and jerk? Did your kite ever get caught in a tree? Were you angry or sad? How did you get it down? How do you bring your kite down from the sky? Can several children fly their kites in the field where you are? What do you wear? What else is in the field? Is there a fence, a hill, a building, or a road nearby?

Draw a picture about flying kites. Make your kite any shape that you would like.

On the Spot . . . Actual Object . . . Bicycle

I Am Riding My Bicycle

Who has ridden a bicycle? Will you show us how you do it? How do you get on? I'll hold it up while you sit on it so we can all see how you are sitting. In what position are your knees? Where are your feet placed? Where do you hold on? What happens to your elbows? How do you hold your head, especially if you are going fast or going uphill or pedalling into the wind? What muscles get tired when you go uphill? Do you ever stand up on the pedals and pump? Is your back straight or at an angle? What clothes do you usually wear? How is a boy's bike different from a girl's? Did you ever fall? Did you ever race with your friends? Do you ever coast downhill? How do you pedal? Are both pedals down at the same time or is one up and one down? Where do you ride your bike? Which street or place will you choose to show in your picture? What buildings are nearby? Do you like to ride around the block? What trees, roads, fences, mailboxes, traffic signs, or what else will be in your picture? Did you ever ride up a hill and get out of breath? Did you ever ride in the rain or on a hot day? When do you go riding on your bike?

Draw yourself riding a bicycle.

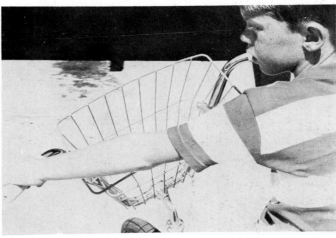

HORSE AND RIDER, Marino Marini
Courtesy of: Collection, The Museum of Modern Art, New York
Acquired through the Lillie P. Bliss Bequest

On the Spot . . . Actual Object . . . Saddle

I AM RIDING A HORSE

Have all of you thought about how much fun it would be to have your very own horse and saddle? Who likes to ride a horse? What color would you like your horse to be? What would you name him? Who can come show us how to sit on this saddle? How do you mount a horse? From which side? (left) Where do you put your hands? When you sit on the saddle with your feet in the stirrups, are your knees bent a little? Are you as tall as a horse? How would you hold the reins? How are your arms bent?

What color is this saddle? Let's touch it and feel how smooth the leather is and how the tooling makes it feel rough where it is decorated. How does it smell? Many people enjoy the spicy odor of leather. What is the horn for? Did you ever see a saddle bag? Where is the cinch? What is a saddle blanket used for? Are you comfortable when you sit in this saddle?

Some horse's manes are long, some are short and clipped. How does the horse's hair feel when you pet him? Did you ever feed a horse a carrot and feel his soft warm nose? Did you ever hear a horse make a neighing sound?

Did you gallop or trot and feel the wind brush your face and blow your hair? Were you wearing a cowboy hat? Did you bounce in the saddle? Did anyone ride with you on another horse? Would you be frightened if the horse bucked? What kind of clothes and boots would you like to wear when you ride? Where would you like to ride?

Draw a picture about you or someone riding a horse.

On the Spot . . . Actual Object . . .
Pair of Roller Skates
I Am Roller Skating

Who can show us how to fasten these roller skates on his feet? Where are the wheels on these skates? What keeps them on your feet? What kind of noise do skates make? Do you stand up straight or bend over when you skate? What does "gliding" mean? How do you go faster and faster? Did you ever fall? Could you skate without bending your knees? Do your arms help you keep your balance? What do you wear when you skate? Do you skate with friends? Where? Did anyone ever skate backwards? Do you like to skate downhill? Do you like to race or skate very fast?

Make a picture about roller skating. Would your picture fit the page better if you draw it vertically on the paper?

On the Spot . . . Actual Object . . . American Flag
I Am Carrying the Flag

Flags have been used for many, many years. Soldiers in ancient times could tell where their leaders were because the leader carried a tall pole with an emblem at the top. The Mohammedans first had the idea of fastening flags to the side of a pole, and the expression "with flags flying" still means things are going well.

Almost every country has a flag of its own and each has a meaning. The thirteen stripes of our flag stand for the thirteen colonies that were our first states. The stars in the blue part stand for the fifty states. George Washington explained the meaning of the colors in this way: the stars and blue union are from heaven; the red is from the mother country, the white stripes separating the red into stripes showing that we are separated from the mother country. The white stripes represent liberty.

Have you ever carried a flag? Where? Perhaps you were a color bearer in a parade. Did it make you feel very proud that you were chosen to carry the flag? Did you stand straight and tall? Was it a tall pole? Did the wind blow and make the flag ripple? How did you hold it? Where were your hands? Come and show us. (The teacher chooses one child to hold the flag.) See where his hands are? Could he hold the flag without bending his elbows? Could he hold the flag with only one hand? Do you suppose the flag would grow heavy if you walked very far with it while the wind is blowing? Is the flag taller than you are?

How might you be dressed to be in a parade? What would be on your head? On your feet? Some children who carry our colors wear Scout uniforms. Other people wear band uniforms or special cowboy outfits. What else? Might you even ride on a horse and carry the flag?

Draw yourself carrying a flag.

On the Spot . . . Actual Object . . . Umbrella and Rainboots
WALKING IN THE RAIN WITH AN UMBRELLA AND BOOTS

Who has walked in the rain with an umbrella? Where did you walk? Was it cold? How were you dressed for a rainy day? What did you put on your feet? Did you wear mittens or gloves? What color was your raincoat? Did you wear something on your head? Did you open your umbrella in the house or after you stepped outside? How did you open it? Who could show us? (The teacher can ask a child to demonstrate.) Could you hold the umbrella over your head without bending your elbow? How did you hold the umbrella when you walked? (The teacher can have a child do this.) See where his hands are so that the wind can't tug and pull the umbrella out of his grip. Is the umbrella over his head? Do you suppose a strong wind could catch inside the umbrella and flip it inside out? Would you need two hands to keep from losing it then?

Do you like to stomp in puddles and make them splash? How are summer rains different from winter rains? If you forgot your raincoat and got soaked through, how did it feel? What shape is the umbrella? What color is it? Does yours have a design or pattern on it? What shape is the handle? What do you smell on a rainy day? What do you hear? When raindrops ping on the umbrella, how does it sound? When a car passes you, what happens to the puddles in the street? Did you ever stick out your tongue and taste the fresh raindrops? Do you like to have water on your face? Does it run down in trickles and drip off your nose? What color are your rain boots? Do they come up to your knees? Do your feet feel larger when you are wearing them? Are they difficult to put on and take off over your shoes?

Draw yourself walking in the rain carrying your umbrella and wearing your boots.

Here and Now . . . Spontaneous Situations

Spontaneous — Unforced, natural, impromptu, offhand, unpremeditated, spur of the moment, extemporaneous, current

When children are excited about an event or occurrence that they have just witnessed or in which they have participated, it is a "here and now" situation and one that can help them to develop their powers of visual communication. The lesson plan may have to be revised to take advantage of a "here and now," but the enthusiastic response of the children will generally warrant this kind of change.

These events are sometimes awaited and prepared for in advance, while other situations arise which are unplanned, unexpected, and which occur to the great delight and interest of the entire class. Both planned and spontaneous happenings strengthen the child's awareness of details and the child's emotional responding. Verbal interchange is also necessary to sum up specific details following the event and preceding the art activity, but this again should be kept at a minimum so that the enthusiasm of the children will not diminish before the art activity begins.

Here and Now
We Played in the Snow Today

How deep was the snow? Were your feet cold? Did any snow get inside your boots? Did you fall down? What is your sled like? Is it saucer shaped or is it on runners? Did you pull it up the hill with a rope? Did your friend or your father pull you? How did you like coasting down the hill? Did you eat any of the fresh snow? Did you see any animal tracks? Did the tree trunks look dark and wet against the white snow? Did any snow stay on the tree branches? Did you see any icicles? How did you dress? Did your ears and nose get cold? Is it hard or easy to walk in deep snow? Who made a snowman? How did you do it? How tall was he when you finished him? Did you make a face for him? Did you ever go skiing or bobsledding?

Draw a picture about what you did in the snow today.

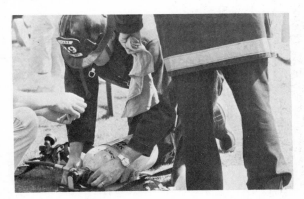

Here and Now

A house or grass fire occurs within viewing dis-
tance of the school. While this occurrence happens
only rarely, the approach to similar highly exciting
topics would involve the same querying approach to
the child's perceptual, intellectual, and emotional responses. The children's fears, apprehensions, tensions,
and excitement would have a ready outlet following
such an experience in an art activity.

A FIRE TRUCK ON THE JOB

The fire trucks have returned to the station now
after the fire. What was the most exciting thing you
remember? The sirens were close to us and were very
loud. We smelled the smoke and saw great billows
of it. What do you remember about the fire trucks?
Where did they keep the hose and how did they put
out the fire? How did the fireman get on top of the
roof? What was he wearing? How was his hat shaped?
What kind of coat was he wearing? Did you see the
flashing light on the truck? What do you suppose
all the dials and handles and little wheels on the side
panel of the truck were for? What color was the roof
after it burned? Were you frightened? Would you
like to be a fireman someday?

Draw a picture about the firemen putting out the
fire.

Here and Now

Most communities have an annual celebration commemorating some historical event. These local occurrences offer exciting possibilities for young children to explore with paint, paper, and crayon. It is history reborn, lore of former times brought to real life in a way that intrigues and inspires children's imaginations as to what life was like long ago. If children can't attend as a group, many will go with their families. Teachers can collect photos in local papers and keep a file of them from year to year to remind the youngsters of what they saw. The photos shown here depict a reenactment of the early pioneers arriving at Sutter's Fort in Sacramento, California.

Pioneer Days (Historical Pageant)

Would you like to have been a little boy or girl when the real pioneers traveled across the hills and valleys in covered wagons? Do you suppose it took them longer than it does us in our cars? Would you have walked along the side or ridden upon a seat in the wagon and helped your father with the mules? What kind of clothes did those children wear? What kind of clothes did the men wear? Would you have liked a coonskin cap? What did you notice about the harnesses on the mules? What color was the canvas cover on the wagons? How big were the wagons? How large were the wheels? Where do you suppose the pioneers ate? How did they cook? Do you think the food smelled good while it was cooking? Did the people stop at night to rest and sleep? What might happen if the Indians weren't friendly? Did some of the pioneers ride bareback, or did they have saddles? What did the saddles look like? How is a cowboy hat different from a Mexican sombrero? How did the women and little girls dress? Do you suppose they got tired? Do you suppose the pioneers took a bath every night? Where did they get their water? What part of the celebration did you like the best? Do you suppose the pioneers were happy when they finally arrived at Sutter's Fort and found friends waiting for them?

Draw a picture about the pioneers and their wagons and mules and how they traveled in the early days.

Here and Now

THE BALLOON PARADE

Did you ever blow up a balloon? How would you like to blow up one of the big balloons that you saw in the parade? The people doing this use air pumps, and it takes a lot of air to fill one of them.

What were some of the figures you saw in the Balloon Parade? Which was the longest? Which was the largest? How was it painted? Which was the tallest? Was it as tall as a building? Was it as wide as the street? Could you put one inside your house?

How did the balloons move along the street? Do you suppose they are very difficult to pull? What were the ropes for?

Which was the funniest? Did any of them almost look alive? Did any of them have sharp edges or were they all soft, rounded shapes?

Draw or paint the balloon that was your favorite in the parade.

Here and Now

Road Machines and Workers

How many words can you think of to describe the big machines that are installing the sewer tiles on our street? What animals do they remind you of? Why? How large are the tires? Are they as tall as you are? What are the different pieces of equipment doing? They are digging, scraping, shoving, filling, packing, pounding, lifting, and wetting down dust. What else? Would you like to drive one of those machines? Which one? Why? Do you think it would be a hard job? What did the men operating the machines wear? What was on the head of each workman? Why? Did you like the dust or mud? What kind of noises did you hear when the machines were working? Where did the men sit? What do you suppose the little umbrella was for? What kind of pattern was on the big tires? Did you see the kind of track it left in the soft earth? What colors were the machines? Did you see the steering wheel and knobs and shifts and pedals? Could you smell fuel burning? Do you feel large or small when you are near one of those pieces of machinery? Which one was the most interesting to you?

Make a picture with cut and torn paper about the machines and the workers.

THE FLOWER VENDOR, Diego Rivera
Courtesy of: Collection, San Francisco Museum of Art
            Gift of Albert M. Bender
            Memorial to Caroline Walter

Images of Myself . . . Emphasis: Figure Drawing
(PHOTO)

By emphasizing one bodily part at a time, this group of motivations nurtures the child's awareness of the physical details of the human figure. This awareness aids in the child's visual interpretation of the human figure.

The degree of self-projection that is reached in many motivations is highly relevant to the flexibility with which the young child deals with the symbol for the human form which he has developed. The concentration of details on stressed parts, the fluency with which he can draw many different configurations, the eloquence he has at his command in changing his own schema, and the ease he shows in exaggerating the significant motions, give coherence, clarity, and spirit to his drawing, painting, and modeling.

Remaining general in scope in a figure drawing motivation leaves the child's art vague and indefinite. Confidence in depicting the human figure flourishes on the building up of carefully structured motivations in which one bodily part or kinesthetic motion is featured as the prime resource for exploration.

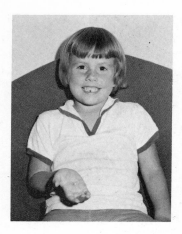

Images of Myself . . . Teeth
I Lost a Tooth

How old were you when you lost your first tooth? Did you pull it or did someone else? What did you use to pull it? String, fingers, pliers? Did it bleed? Did you put it under your pillow for the tooth fairy or did you put it in your baby book? Could you put your tongue in the empty space where your tooth was? Did you miss your tooth when you tried to bite something? Did it hurt when you first pulled it? Had you wiggled it with your tongue for days and days before it finally came out? Did you look at yourself in the mirror to see how you looked without your tooth?

Draw a picture of yourself showing how you looked and felt when you lost your first tooth.

Images of Myself . . . Face
I Am Wearing Dark Glasses

How does the world look through dark glasses? Why do people wear them? What shape are glasses? Are all dark glasses the same shape? How do you keep them from falling off? Put your thumb on the tip of your nose and your forefinger on your eyebrow and then move both over to your ear. Did you find that your nose is about as long as your ear and about even with your nose and eyes? Did you ever have a pair of dark glasses that pinched your nose too tightly? Do you like to wear dark glasses? Did you ever look at yourself in a mirror while you were wearing them?

Draw yourself wearing dark glasses.

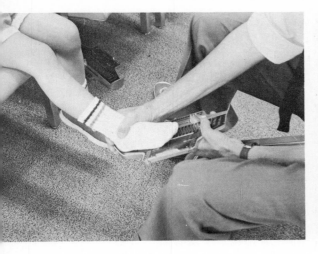 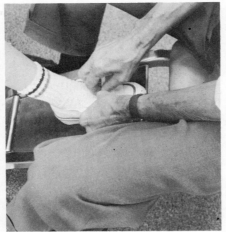

Images of Myself . . . Feet
BUYING NEW SHOES

Can you remember the last time your parents bought you a new pair of shoes? Where did you go? How are the chairs arranged in a shoe store? Did you sit or stand when the man in the store fitted your feet? How did he fit them? What did he use? Did he sit or stand in front of you? Can you remember your shoe size? Did you leave your socks on for the fitting? How many pairs of shoes did he have you try before you decided which ones were the best? Did some feel too tight or too large? Did they tie or buckle or button or slip on? Did you walk down the aisle to see how they felt? Were they a bit stiff? What color of shoes did you finally buy? Did you wear them out of the store or carry them in a box? Were the soles rubber? Were the shoes easy to slide on? Did they have a "new shoe" smell? Did you get a blister the first time you wore them? Did you feel as if you could jump higher and run faster when you wore them?

Draw yourself buying a new pair of shoes.

Images of Myself . . . Ear and Face
LISTENING TO A SECRET

What is a secret? Why are secrets so much fun? How do you tell your best friend a secret? Would it be a secret if you told a lot of people? Do you tell secrets out loud or do you whisper? Do you like your best friend to tell you a secret? How does a whisper feel in your ear? Can you remember if your ear felt tickly when your friend whispered into it? Does it make you giggle? Could you hear your friend if he stood across the room and whispered? Can you hear him if he stands very close and whispers right into your ear?

Draw yourself listening to your friend whisper a secret into your ear.

WOMAN HOLDING COMB, Torii Kiyomasu
Courtesy of: The Art Institute of Chicago
Clarence Buckingham collection

Images of Myself . . . Hair
I AM HAVING MY HAIR COMBED

How long is your hair? Do you wear it hanging long, straight, or curled? Is it ever braided? Do you have bangs? On which side is your hair parted? What color is your hair? Do you comb your own hair or does your mother or sister or grandmother sometimes do it? What kind of comb is used? Do you sit or stand to have your hair combed? Is it ever tangled? Does it hurt to pull out the snarls? Do you use a brush to make your hair shine? Does your scalp tingle when you are through having it brushed?

Draw yourself having your hair combed.

Images of Myself . . . Neck
I Am Wearing My New Necktie

How is a bowtie different from a long neck tie? Which do you have? Do you wear it every day or just for special dress-up occasions? What color is it? Is it striped or plain? Do you wear it with a white shirt or with a colored shirt? How does it fit under your collar? Is your collar pointed, rounded, or button-down? What length are your shirt sleeves? Does your collar ever feel too tight around your neck? If you look down, can you see your tie? What color are the pants you wear? Do you like to wear your tie?

Draw yourself wearing your new necktie.

Images of Myself . . . Shoulders and Arms
I Am Hanging by My Arms

Who can put his arms high above his head and stretch? Look up. Can you pretend that there is a tree branch or an acting bar above you? Did you ever hold tightly and hang by your arms? Were your fingers curled away from you or toward you? Did your arms begin to ache after you hung there for awhile? How did your armpits feel? How far below you was the ground? Did you drop down when you let go? Did you ever swing yourself along a branch or a bar one hand over the other? Did it help to swing your body and legs back and forth to help you propel yourself along? Can anyone chin himself? That means to lift yourself up until your chin touches the bar. Would you bend your elbows if you did this? Did you ever lift your legs up and turn yourself "inside out"? How long can you hang by your arms before you let go? Do your arms feel longer and longer as you hang there? Where have you hung by your arms? What was below you, above you? What were you wearing? Who was playing with you?

Draw yourself hanging by your arms.

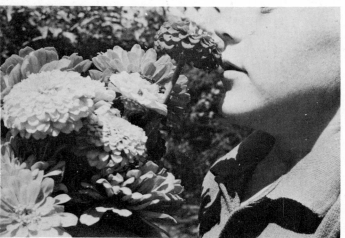

Images of Myself . . . Knees and Hands
WE ARE PLAYING MARBLES OR JACKS

Who can show us how you play marbles or jacks? How are the two games alike? Both have to be played on the ground, and we must kneel to be in the best position. Do your knees ever get tired? Do you wear out your jeans if you play on the ground quite often. Do you bend over to shoot the marbles? Do you sit up straight or lean a little to bounce the jack ball? Do you sit back on your feet or do your legs go straight up from your knees? Where do you play marbles or jacks? Do you play with your friends in a circle around the ring? How many marbles do you have? Do you keep your marbles or jacks in a little drawstring bag? How do you hold the marble to shoot it? Why is your thumb important? Do you put your hand on the ground to shoot? When you play jacks, how do you bounce the ball? While the ball is in the air what do you do with your hand? How do you hold your hand to catch the ball? Do you ever miss the ball? Do you ever miss a shot when you play marbles? Are you angry or disappointed when you do?

Draw yourself and your friends kneeling to play marbles or jacks.

Images of Myself . . . Nose
I AM SNIFFING A FLOWER

Do all flowers have a fragrant smell? Which ones do you like to smell? How large are they? Are they as large as your hand? Were the petals on each flower all one color or different colors? What was in the middle of the flower? Did you get any of the yellow pollen dust on your nose when you sniffed? Did you put your head down to sniff the blossoms or did you pick the flower and hold it in your hand? Would you be able to smell a flower if your nose were stopped up? What is the shape of your nose? Do you know where your "nostrils" are? Feel where you nose starts between your eyes and goes down to the tip, and then find your nostrils. Squeeze your nose with your fingers. Wrinkle your nose. Does it feel larger than normally when you do this? Take two or three sniffs and pretend that you are smelling a flower.

Draw yourself sniffing a flower.

Images of Myself . . . Legs and Feet

I Am Playing Hopscotch

Hopscotch is a very, very old game. Children all over the world play some sort of hopscotch. How many different kinds do you know? Do you draw hopscotch with chalk on the sidewalk or scratch it with a stick in hard earth? How do you hop? On one foot? Do you bend your other knee to hold your leg off the ground? How do you jump from one square to the next? Do you bend over when you jump? Do you jump on your toes or flat footed? How far can you jump? Do your arms help you? How? What do you wear when you play? Do you play with several friends? How do you feel when you miss? Do you mind if you win or lose?

Draw a picture about children playing hopscotch.

TEACHER'S NOTE:

RIMBLES, a book of children's classic games, rhymes, songs, and sayings, by Patricia Evans, is a rich source of rules and drawings of hopscotch variations which children will delight in learning. Brief historical background is included.

Divergent Paths . . . Related Topics for . . .
DIRECT HAPPENINGS

Verbal Interchange

We are playing pirates; We are playing Eskimos; We are playing cowboys; My birthday gift from Grandmother; I am riding my skateboard; I am riding a surfboard; I am fishing from a boat, I am fishing through a hole in the ice; We are going hunting; This is my family all dressed up; Having our photograph taken; Watching the fireworks display

On Location

We watched workers building a house, Men repairing the street; The tree trimmers; We visit the post office, the bakery, the park, the airport, the fish hatchery, the train station, the doughnut shop, the fire station, the greenhouse; We take a bus ride

Acting-It-Out

Daddy mowing the grass; I am setting the table; I am helping build a fire; I am helping wash the car; I am planting seeds; I am raking leaves; I am wading in the creek; I am chopping wood; I am square dancing; I am playing golf; Walking with crutches or cane; I am shooting a bow and arrow

On the Spot . . . Actual Object

Bouncing a ball; Playing dodge ball; Playing kick ball; Batting a ball; Playing tether ball; Playing handball; I am riding a tricycle; Saluting the flag; Putting flags on graves of soldiers on Memorial Day; I am ice skating; I am tap dancing; I twirl a baton; I am eating an apple, banana, taffy, watermelon

Here and Now . . . Spontaneous Happenings

What the strong wind did; A car accident on the corner; An ambulance on the job; We planted a tree on Arbor Day; The Magician we saw today; The animal that visited our class

Images of Myself

I am chewing hard candy; I am eating corn on the cob; I am talking on the telephone; I have a black eye; I am crying tears; Buying a new hat; My new gloves or jewelry; When I wore finger nail polish; I have an earache; Listening to a seashell; I am having my hair curled; My beautiful hair ribbons; I am hanging by my knees; I am screaming; I am whistling; I am taking medicine; When I had a sore throat; My nosebleed; I have a freckled nose; Kneeling before the King; Saying prayers; Pushing my toy truck; Planting bulbs; I have a new cowboy belt; My new bathing suit; My new red apron

Roundabout Happenings...
Dialogues with Aids

Roundabout — indirect, circuitous, all maner of ways

Roundabout motivations, through the use of audio and visual means, bring the rich, outside world into focus for a close, comprehensive scrutiny by the child. These vicarious happenings might otherwise remain remote and impersonal were it not for such devices that make possible the child's strong involvement and self-identification. For example, a film on spiders gives emotional impact and enlarges isolated details. Time lapse photography presents a new understanding of the designs in plant life. Children living in warm climates find identifying with winter adventures much easier after viewing a film strip about snow and ice. Poems quickly stimulate delightful mental images. Books expand topics in many areas of thought. Photographs and slides present many facets of one subject, focus on small details which might otherwise be overlooked, and bring far away or moving objects close for thorough investigation.

The teacher's role in the use of roundabout devices is that of providing a verbal interchange in which provocative questions engage the child's thoughts in a direct and personal connection with the subject being presented.

Films and Film Strips

Some of the most effective and stimulating motivational methods are those involving the use of films and film strips.

The screen on which these visual aids are projected frames, isolates, and focuses on subject matter in such a manner that is unique and impossible to do even if the real object or place were available for viewing or visiting. The use of microphotography, close-up, time-lapse photography, telephoto shots, and underwater camera angles presents views of nature and scientific phenomena which develop in the child a sense of the order and aesthetic design of the universe. Enlarged shots reveal designs, shapes, colors, and textures that might go unnoticed if seen only in the natural world.

Film strips permit the children to view a single panel for as long as they wish or to return to it to find answers to their questions. Film strips composed of color photographs are superior for art motivational purposes to those employing drawings.

While the scientific or social studies aspects are not to be overlooked, discussion for an art motivation should emphasize points relating to emotional appeal, color, design, arrangement, shapes, and textures. Questions that help the children project themselves into the film, that help them pinpoint the part which interests them most and that guide them in deciding how they are going to present that part visually in paint, crayon or other media are paramount.

All or only part of the film or film strip may be shown depending on its appropriateness, its length, and the interest span of the class. It is not wise to bombard the very young with too many stimulating aspects at one viewing. The sound track may be turned off in some instances. These are decisions to be made by the teacher during a preview of the material.

It is strongly recommended that the teacher preview each film or film strip before showing it to the class. Then he can decide whether it meets the specific purpose for which it is intended and whether it meets standards of artistic planning and preparation.

Film: Circus's Coming . . . . **International Film Bureau**

(If a child has not had the opportunity to see a circus and has only seen brief snatches of what one is like through books, television, or posters, or if the child has actually attended a real circus, this film will unify and revitalize his concepts of a circus. Sounds, smells, excitement, tastes, color, all are suggested in this film. The camera moves over a miniature model of a circus. A few portions of the film are animated. Close-ups enable the child to comprehend details in a way that is stimulating and understandable.)

What did we see first? We saw the painted wagons on railroad cars as they were being unloaded, and the men driving stakes to set up the many tents. What were these odd job men called? (Roustabouts) A circus is almost like a traveling town; it has its own hospital tent, blacksmith shop, dining tent, barber shop, and the costume tent with all the brightly colored satins and silks and spangles. Would you like to have the job of hauling water to elephants? What do you remember about the circus parade scene in this film? (Flags, plumes on the horses' heads, bandwagon, the brightly colored uniforms or the musicians as the band rode on the red and gold wagon) Where have you heard a calliope? How do you feel when you hear one? Have you ever been in crowds?

Do you remember the dust and noise of the circus? How did you like the side shows, the sword swallower, the strong man? When you go to the circus, do you like to eat cotton candy, hot dogs and drink pink lemonade? If you buy balloons and pennants, be sure to save enough money for a ticket into the Big Top and the menagerie tent. Did you see the elephants reaching for peanuts in the menagerie tent? Did you see the giraffes, the llamas, camels, gorillas, and chimps? Where were some of the ferocious animals? (Cage wagons) What holds up the Big Top? How were the girls on the elephants dressed? What was the tight rope walker doing? Do you remember the bright blankets on the elephants? Do you think it would be hard to swing by your teeth at the top of the tent? What else did you see? Do you remember the bear on a scooter with an umbrella; the flying trapeze on the playground; the bareback riders standing on the horses? How do you think it would feel to stand on a horse when it galloped? Clowns are almost always a favorite. What tricks were they doing? What were the elephants and the girls doing that was scarey?

Which part of the circus would you like to draw in a picture? Or which performer or animal could you model with clay?

CIRCUS ELEPHANTS, John Marin
Courtesy of: The Art Institute of Chicago
Robert A. Waller fund and Alfred Stieglitz collection

Film

INSECT CATCHERS OF THE BOG JUNGLE

Did you ever think that a flower could catch an insect? Can you describe some of the unusual and different shapes the flowers were? Do you remember the long spikes that the one had with which to grasp its food? Were all of the colors bright? Did the flowers look strong? Do you suppose the insides of some of the flowers were as sticky as honey? Do you suppose the insect smelled the flower and that is how he found it? Did the inside of one of the flowers look as slippery as your slide on the playground? Can insects swim? What shapes and colors were the insects? How many insects do you think a hungry flower could eat? How large will you have to make your flower in order to show all the details of the inside of the flower and of the insect? Will you make your flower look inviting to the insect? Could you make the flower look mean and hungry by your selection of color and texture and shape without showing a face on it?

Draw a flower catching an insect.

Film

SPIDER ENGINEERS . . . MOODY INSTITUTE OF SCIENCE

How did it feel to see a spider on the screen that was as large as you are? Did he frighten you or do you think he would make a good playmate? How do you think it would feel to have eight legs? Did the spiders have hairy or smooth legs? Was one part of the body bigger than the other? Were all the spiders the same colors? What color spiders have you seen? Have you ever seen a trap door spider? How do you think it would feel to live underground? The spider must have strong legs to dig in the ground. Did you ever try to dig in the hard ground with your fingers? How would you like to walk about on a springy net and keep track of all eight legs? How would you like to live under water? How many different ways did the spiders have of getting their food?

Draw the idea you have of a large spider.

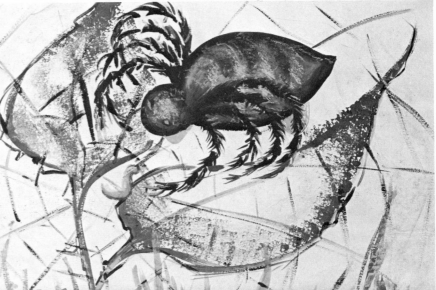

Film Strip

The film, *Animals to Know*, shows many sizes, shapes, and kinds of animals. Some shots are of mothers with their young, others show animals eating in the zoo or in their natural habitat. The pictures are clear and close-up, showing the animals in good detail. Some of the animals will be quite familiar, others may need an introduction.

ANIMALS TO KNOW . . . A ROW-PETERSON TEXTFILM

Animal mothers love their babies and care for them while they are growing. What do you remember seeing these mothers do for their young? Have you seen other animal mothers taking care of their babies at the zoo? What were some of the ways these mothers carried their babies? Would you like to be carried like that? Which two animals would be best to stay away from? Why? Which animals live in the cold, snow country? How do they stay warm? Which animal was the funniest? Which had the most beautiful pattern on its back? Which was a good swimmer? Would you like to swim as well as he does? What did that pile of alligators make you think of? Did you know that so many animals had stripes? Some animals had soft fur, some long manes. How many kinds of tails did you see? Which animal was the heaviest? Did he have the biggest mouth? Do you suppose camels get tired carrying humps on their backs? Why do you suppose we say, "proud as a peacock?" Which animals had feathers? Would you like to sleep like a bat? Which animals were shown laying eggs?

Which animal would you choose for your picture or for clay modeling?

Film Strip

An American Farmer . . . Encyclopedia Britannica Films

What is the big difference in farmers of today and those of about 100 years ago? Would you rather live on a farm or in the city? Why? What did the different machines you just saw do? Would you like to help operate one of them? Which one? How large do you think the tractor was? What was the shape of it? What color? Which animals did you see on the film strip? Why do some farmers raise a lot of corn? Where do they store it? How are cows milked? Did you ever go to a farm? How is hay put in the barn? What colors of barns have you seen? What are trucks used for on a farm? Did you ever watch a farmer plow a field and turn over the soil? What color is corn when it's growing? How tall does it grow? What kind of fruit was grown in the orchard in the film strip? What kind of fruit is grown where we live? How is it picked and shipped and stored? Did you ever walk in an orchard when it was in bloom in the spring? How did it smell? Did you ever climb a tree and pick an apple or a peach or an apricot? How do farmers dress when they work?

Suggested Topics:
Draw the farmer operating one of the machines.
Draw the farmer milking the cows.
Draw the farmer using a truck.
Draw the farmer working in the orchard.
Draw the farmer working in the corn field.

Books

Books hold between their covers many clues that can serve to evoke the child's imagination. They are rich and varied sources upon which to base an art motivation.

Since books deal with subjects verbally as well as visually, they present a wealth of sensations that a cursory observation of the same phenomena in nature might not take into account. From both the factual information and sensory impressions, the child expresses artistic structures in his art product with a freshness uniquely his own.

When photographs from a book are shown to the children, they should be used *only* during the verbal interchange and then should be put away while the children are involved in the actual art process. Particular photographs and factual clues pertinent to the motivational task should be selected before the art period.

Book

This book of kittens and cats is a collection of over 240 photographs of cats. It shows them from birth throughout life in a wide range of activities. Some are house pets, some are show cats, alley cats, kittens full of mischief. In short, cats are depicted in a style that will appeal to children, that will remind them of cats they have known or would like to own. The photos are large enough so that the book could be held in front of a group of children.

WALTER CHANDOHA'S BOOK OF KITTENS AND CATS . . .
THE CITADEL PRESS, NEW YORK

Did you ever hold a newborn kitten like this one? Were its eyes open? How big was it? How did it get its milk before it learned to drink from a saucer?

How did the mother give it a bath? Would you like that kind of bath? How do kittens hold their tails when they walk? How do they sleep? How do they play? Did you ever feel a kitten's paws? What are their noses like? Can you curl up like a cat . . . stretch like a cat?

Would you like to have whiskers like a cat does? Would you like to lap up milk and eat your meals without your hands as this one is doing? See the milk on his whiskers.

What kind of noises do cats make? How do cats act around dogs? What colors of cats have you known?

Why does a cat purr? Do cats ever get angry? Are they curious? Did you ever see cats fight or play together? What shape are cats' eyes? Did you ever play with a striped cat or with one with white paws? How is a Siamese cat different from other cats? How is a cat's nose shaped? Can you hear a cat walking?

What sort of teeth does a cat have? How does a mother cat carry her young? Does your cat sleep in a special basket?

What can you tell us about cats and kittens in your picture? Can you model a cat?

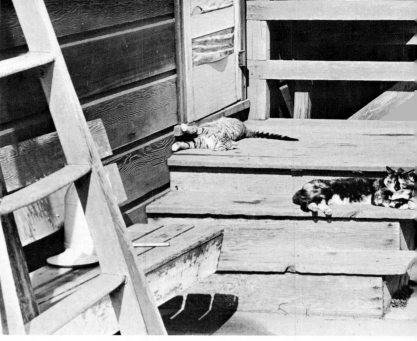

Photo Credit: Shirley

SUGGESTED TOPICS for DRAWING, PAINTING, and MODELING:

Cat lapping milk
Mother nursing her kittens
Cats playing
Angry cat
Mothers carrying kittens
Mothers washing kittens
Sleeping cat
A cat purring

Photo Credit: Shirley Poirier

CLOWN, Georges Rouault
Courtesy of: Collection, The Museum of Modern Art, New York
Gift of Vladimir Horowitz

Book

Clowns Through the Ages is a gay history of clowning, wandering over the world from China to India, Europe, and America and from the courts of the Pharaohs to the three-ring circus. It shows how clowning developed both in palaces and in market-places. It tells of Medieval merry makers — of jesters and merry-councillors, of gleemen and mummers; and of more modern ones — the white-faced clowns and Augustes, clowns of harlequinades and pantomimes, theater and circus, great legendary mischief-makers and familiar favorites we all know.

The last chapters are the most useable for primary children in that they deal with verbal descriptions and interesting stories about the classic types of clowns.

CLOWNS THROUGH THE AGES *by John Hornby* . . . HENRY Z. WALCK, INC., THE BYWAYS LIBRARY

Clowns have long been a favorite subject for children and grown-up artists to draw and paint and model — perhaps because they wear such colorful and unusual costumes and have funny expressions painted on their faces and do so many comical acts such as falling off a mule, blowing smoke out of their ears, or walking around with a trained dog or bear. What tricks have you seen clowns do? Can you remember how they were dressed?

Did you know that clowns have been performing for thousands of years? A long time ago in 1823, a clown in New York loved horses. He wore riding boots and red and white tights that made his legs look extra long. He wore a top hat and a beard and smoked a cigar. He looked mean, but he was a kind man and was a friend of Abe Lincoln. The clown pretended to fall off his horse, but, of course, he was a marvelous rider.

Two Russian clowns used rats and a pig in their act. One of these brothers dressed up as the Pied Piper, and hundreds of the trained rats answered the call of his

Children worked in groups of four to construct large life-size clowns. The clothing was made with paint, crayon, colored paper, and pieces of fabric. Potato and art gum prints added an interesting pattern.

pipe by swarming all over him. His pet pig was named Chuska, and he trained this pig to descend from a balloon with a parachute.

Grock was a famous clown who worked with a clever white-faced clown called Antonet. Grock wore a huge overcoat and boots big enough for a giant, white gloves so large that when he and Antonet played the piano or violin, the fingers and thumbs flopped all over.

Coco was loved in Britain. He had a round, red nose, a tiny mouth, and huge eyebrows. He wore a checked suit, and he made people laugh by getting soaked with buckets of water.

Some clowns perform on a wire or a trapeze. They pretend to fall and always save themselves at the last minute.

Emmet Kelly, who was known as Weary Willy, was a famous American clown. His clothes were made of rags, and he wore a battered hat. He looked very sad and never said a word. Some clowns walk around on high stilts with pants covering them so that they seem to be as tall as a house. Some clowns ride enormous bicycles.

If you could be any kind of clown, which would you be? How would you dress? If you could see any of these clowns, which would you like to watch? Think of the shoes, the pants, the coat, the funny face, the hat. What colors will you use? What will you have your clown doing to make people laugh? Where will the clown be performing? Who will be watching him? Will any other clowns be doing anything with him? Will he need an animal in his act?

SUGGESTED TOPICS for DRAWING, PAINTING and MODELING
   A clown I saw
   The clown I would like to be
   A funny thing a clown did
   A family of clowns

Book

Dogs Dogs Dogs By *Paul Hamlyn* . . . London

Dogs have been friends of man for thousands of years. Husky teams helped explore the polar regions, and dogs circled the earth in space before human astronauts ventured forth. Dogs are rescue workers in high mountains, and they have served in the Army. Sportsmen have dogs to help them hunt, and guide dogs lead blind people. Dogs herd cattle, run races, and make wonderful pets, too. Dogs come in all shapes, colors, and sizes. This book has many photographs of dogs as well as drawings and paintings and pieces of sculpture of dogs which were done by famous adult artists.

Some dogs look as if they would be good playmates. Some look just plain frisky and sassy and full of pep, and some look very snooty. What is it about a dog that makes him look sad and dejected?

Some dogs are neatly clipped or short haired and some have long silky hair. Some of the dogs' ears are upright and pointed and some are long and droopy.

Which dog has the longest legs? Which has the shortest? Look at how many different kinds of tails there are. Some dogs are spotted, some all one color.

How does a dog pant? Why do dogs wag their tails? What do retrievers do?

Did you ever walk a dog on a leash? Did the dog pull you along? Can you run as fast as your own dog can run? Greyhound dogs run races on race tracks.

Did you ever teach a dog a trick? What sort of trick? Did you ever enter a dog in a dog show?

How do you care for *your* dog? What sort of a dog would you *like* to have if you don't already have a dog?

Draw a picture about that kind of dog.

MINIATURE FIGURE OF A DOG, Egyptian
Courtesy of: The Metropolitan Museum of Art
Rogers Fund, 1947

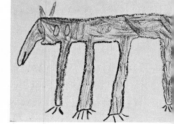

Book

HORSES HORSES HORSES BY *Paul Hamlyn* . . . LONDON

Horses are strong, fast-running, beautiful, intelligent, and generally friendly. No wonder so many people love them. Horses have helped and aided man in many ways by plowing his fields, carrying him from one place to another, bearing him to battle, racing, jumping, performing in circuses, and acting in television and films.

If you could be a horse, which kind of horse would you choose? Here are some pictures of various types of horses doing different things.

Suggested pictures to show:
The Thoroughbred. . . a handsome fast running horse
Arabian show horses
Here are horses in harness, the hackney, high stepping, very fast, works with a partner. See the driver in top hat. What are the blinders for?
How are the dray horse's hoofs different from other horses?
A favorite of children, the Shetland pony
The race horse! See the jockeys lean over and urge their horses to pound around the track faster and faster? How are the race horse's legs when he is running fast? What happens to his tail? How is the race track shaped?
Do you think this horse *Likes* to jump? See his legs, how he holds them to clear the hurdle. Look at his mane and tail. The rider is dressed in special clothes. How are they different from the cowboy's?
Trotting horses
Polo players need a well trained horse to help them win. Would you like to play this game?
Did you ever try to jump a fence or hurdle of some sort? See the riders lean close to the horse's neck. The horse's front legs are bent. Sometimes they are out straight.
And sometimes the rider takes a spill . . . and even the horse!

Long ago, horses pulled stage coaches and worked together in teams.
They plowed fields for farmers.
And some horses carry policemen.
Rodeo horses try to throw off their riders by bucking.
Some rodeo horses help the cowboys rope calves.
Horses are always important in the circus ring.
Horses must be very intelligent and well trained.
Which horse would *you* like to be?
Make a picture about horses.

TEACHER'S NOTE:
After the children are finished drawing, they might be interested in seeing how grown-up artists all over the world since time began have used the horse as subject matter for their art. An excellent review is also presented in this book.

Book

LIVING FISHES OF THE WORLD *by Earl S. Herald* . . .
DOUBLEDAY & CO., GARDEN CITY, NEW YORK

Let's imagine we have a submarine made entirely of *Glass*. What do you think we'll see as we explore the ocean floor? We'll shine our giant floodlight ahead of us and to both sides of us and look for all sorts of fish.

How would you like to live in the sea and be a fish? Which fish would you be? Which of these fishes has the most beautiful pattern on its body? Which is the most ferocious? Which is the largest? What does this electric catfish remind you of?

How is the seahorse different from a regular horse?

Can you find the fins on these spotted and striped fish? What is the shape of the mouth? How do you suppose a little fish feels when he finds himself gobbled up by a big fish?

Some fish are long, some are flat, some are round. Can you tell which is the front end of this longnose butterfly fish? Where do you suppose the queen angelfish got its name? What is unusual about its coloring? Look at the beautiful patterns on the young imperial angelfish. It's easy to see how the clown anemone fish got its name. Would you be able to guess the names of the balloonfish, turkeyfish, puffers, cowfish, and whiskery frogfish?

How is the threadfin fish different from the others?

Here's a whole school of fish. Look at the beautiful Siamese Fighting Fish. Does he remind you of a beautiful ballerina or a princess?

Does the scorpionfish look mean and tough? Some fish are so camouflaged that they are difficult to see on the ocean floor.

Which fishes interested you the most? What shape were they? What colors? Where were they swimming? What kind of personality will your fishes have? How will they be decorated?

Draw the fish that you thought had the most interesting shape and color, or draw a fish that is your own creation.

Poems and Records

Poems and records are especially useful tools for creating a motivation since, by their nature, they provoke highly individualized and imaginative responses. They quickly produce in the child's mind a unique and personal mental image which may be delightful, frightening, exciting, humorous, or sad.

As in all motivations, a personal involvement with the subject matter is essential. Poems and records are especially suitable for young children in that they are short and permit an instant response to pour out in paint, crayon, or clay.

Poems and records that are successfully used for art motivations basically are in two categories, and these two groupings often overlap. One group is composed of those that relate an event or tell a short story, and the other group includes those that create a mood or feeling. Both excite visual concepts in the mind of the child. One type should not be used to the exclusion of the other type.

Poem

A Partridge in a Pear Tree
On the first day of Christmas, my true love gave to me
A Partridge in a pear tree.
On the second day of Christmas, my true love gave to me
Two turtle doves.
On the third day of Christmas, my true love gave to me
Three French hens.

On the fourth day of Christmas, my true love gave to me
Four Collie birds.
On the fifth day of Christmas, my true love gave to me
Five golden rings.
On the sixth day of Christmas, my true love gave to me
Six geese a-laying.
On the seventh day of Christmas, my true love gave to me
Seven swans a-swimming.
On the eighth day of Christmas, my true love gave to me
Eight maids a-milking
On the ninth day of Christmas, my true love gave to me
Nine pipers piping.
On the tenth day of Christmas, my true love gave to me
Ten drummers drumming.
On the eleventh day of Christmas, my true love gave to me
'Leven lords a-leaping.
On the twelfth day of Christmas, my true love gave to me
Twelve ladies dancing.

This is a very old poem, and sometimes we sing it to a lovely melody. As we read it over, did you imagine what some of the things mentioned might look like? Could you show in your painting some of the feelings you had when you heard the words? Which of the things mentioned interested you the most? Many years ago, the words of the poem were sung as part of a game, and if you made a mistake in remembering the words, you had to pay a penalty. The pear tree refers to an old Christmas custom in which a girl would back into a pear tree, circle it three times and would be rewarded by seeing the image of her sweetheart. The four collie birds has to do with coal black hens. The five golden rings mean ringed pheasants.

This is a happy poem. What colors make you feel happy? Perhaps you might want to combine several of the things the poem talks about in your picture, and you even might use numbers as part of your design. A pear tree has many branches and sweet golden fruit. Choose the part or parts of the poem that you like best and draw about it.

Record

"Puff, the Magic Dragon" by *Peter, Paul, and Mary*
. . . A Warner Bros. Record #5348

This is a wonderful folk song about a dragon named Puff. Have any of you ever pretended that you owned an imaginary dragon or any kind of make-believe pet? The little boy in the song was named Jackie Paper and his dragon was named Puff. Where did Puff live? (By the sea) What did Jackie bring the dragon? (Strings, sealing wax, and other fancy stuff) The song says Puff played happily in the autumn mist. Jackie pretended that they took wonderful trips together on a boat with a big, billowing sail while he perched on Puff's tail and kept a lookout. How big do you think Puff must have been? Do you think he was a friendly dragon? How did Puff tell people his name? (Roared it out) Who bowed down? (Noble kings and princes and pirate ships lowered their flags)

What happened to Puff? (Jackie grew up and no longer needed to play with him. When Jackie stopped coming, Puff stopped roaring.) He bent his head down, and his green scales must have fallen like tear drops. He must have been very sad because he slipped into his cave. Let's find Puff! We can pretend he is our own personal magic dragon. What will he look like? How big will he be? How is his head shaped? What color is he? How will you show him puffing? You could pretend to perch on his tail as Jackie did and be on the lookout for pirate ships, or you could take him lovely gifts and sit and talk to him. What else might you do with your dragon?

Draw (or model) Puff, the Magic Dragon.

What other art material could you use to make Puff?

Suggested Topics for Drawing, Painting and Modeling
    Riding Puff, the Magic Dragon
    Bringing gifts to Puff

    Puff scaring Kings and Princes
    Puff going into his cave
    Puff riding on a ship

Record

"The Big Black Hat" *by Rolf Harris* . . .
an Epic 45-rpm record 5-9596.

How would you like to meet a man dressed in the manner described in this record? Would you be frightened, curious, or amused?

Can you remember how the man was dressed — starting with what he wore on his head? What sort of brim did the hat have? What kind of band? How do you imagine the man's moustache was shaped? What sort of glasses were on his nose? What was around his neck and what was attached to it and dragging on the ground? What is a "sunshade"? What color was the man's sunshade, and where did he hold it? What sort of coat and shirt and trousers do you suppose he might have worn? Do you imagine that this strange man was tall or short — fat or thin? Do you think he had large feet or small — wore boots or shoes or sandals?

Draw your idea of how you think this strangely dressed man really looked. Be sure to remember all the odd things he was wearing that were described in the record.

Photograph Collections

Another motivational method that involves strong emphasis on visual awareness is that employing the use of mounted photograph collections. These pictures may be gathered from sources such as newspapers, magazines, and commercial collections. They are best mounted on a light weight tag board for easy storing and for effective viewing. It is important to remember, as in the case of any visual material handled during a motivation, that all photographs be thoroughly viewed and discussed prior to the art activity and that they be put away and not copied while the children work. A single photograph should never be used since a dependent child will try to recall the one picture and draw it during the art activity rather than using the emotional qualities, ideas, and diversified aspects presented in a multiple group of photographs.

Photograph Collection

THINGS WE BLOW

Photo 1. Do you think that Amy will blow out all the candles on her birthday cake with one big breath? Could you?

Photo 2. How do your cheeks feel when you blow up a balloon? Did one ever pop while you were blowing it up? How many shapes of balloons are there?

Photo 3. How large are they when you finish filling them with air? What is your favorite color? How do you hold a balloon while you are blowing it?

Photo 4. Have you ever blown a bubble with bubble gum?

Photo 5. Ronnie blows his windmill hard to make it go around and around. When he stops blowing, the windmill stops, too. What color windmill do you like best?

Photos 6, 7, and 8. What shape of bubble pipe do you use when you blow bubbles? How do you hold it? How do you fill the pipe? Do you blow softly? Can you see sun reflections in the bubble while you are blowing? Do some bubbles break off the pipe and float gently away? Where do bubbles go when they break?

Photo 9. Can you blow up a paper bag and then smash it to make it pop?

Photo 10. Did you ever blow a thistle or a dandelion and watch the soft seeds parachute slowly to the ground?

Draw a picture about blowing something.

Photo 1.

Photo 4.

Photo 5.

Photo 3.

Photo 2.

Photo 6.

Photo 7.

Photo 8.

Photo 9.

Photo 10.

BOY BLOWING BUBBLES, Manet
Courtesy of: Collection of the Calouste Gulbenkian Foundation
Palacio Pombal, Oeiras, Portugal

Courtesy of: Louisville & Nashville Railroad

Courtesy of: Santa Fe Railway

Photograph Collection
RAILROADING

What is a train? A steam, diesel, or electric locomotive to pull all the cars. Passenger cars, freight cars, coal cars, and cars for hauling oil. Double deck commuters and a piggyback express. Auto-racks, coaches, diners, sleepers, baggage, and observation cars. Club, tank cars, flat cars, box cars, stock cars, refrigerator cars, and last of all the caboose.

What is a train? A train is a noise.

Where is a train? In stations, on sidings, or shooting through plains and deserts. Over bridges, through tunnels, climbing mountains, having a shower. On the track, on sidings, of steel, spikes, and wooden ties.

Why is a train? To carry people, freight of all kinds, oil, automobiles, fruit, cattle, sugar beets, grain, rubber, logs, coal, and Uncle Sam's mail.

When is a train? Day and night, summer, winter, spring, and fall. Around the clock, on time, late, or early. When you stand in the station, you can *feel* a train inside your feet.

How is a train? A train is steel, aluminum, iron, elephant-big, red, brown, orange, gray, and silver. Couplings, signals, lights, flagmen, microwaves, semaphores, switches, and crew. Gandy dancers, conductors, and of course, the engineer!

Draw, cut-out, paint, or use a print making procedure to create a long train on a long track. Work alone or with a few friends.

TEACHER'S NOTE:

These photographs may be cut out of the book and be used with the following motivation. Do you know any railroading songs and records?

Courtesy of: Denver & Rio Grande Western Railroad

Courtesy of: Association of American Railroads Washington, D. C.

Courtesy of: Great Northern Railway

Courtesy of: Rock Island Lines

OLD ST. LAZARE STATION, PARIS, Claude Monet

Courtesy of: The Art Institute of Chicago Mr. & Mrs. Martin A. Ryerson collection

Courtesy of: Baltimore and Ohio Railroad

Courtesy of: Association of American Railroads, Washington, D. C.

Courtesy of: Chesapeake & Ohio Railway

Courtesy of: Association of American Railroads Washington, D. C.

Courtesy of: Great Northern Railway

Photograph Collection

RODEO RIDERS

Who has been to a rodeo? Did you know that rodeos began in the early days of the West? Once each year, cowboys rounded up all the cattle that belonged to each ranch owner. Then they

Photo Credit: Rodeo Photographer, Frank Milne

Photo Credit: Rodeo Photographer, Frank Milne

had contests at these roundups to show how good they were at the work they did. The word "rodeo" is Spanish and it means "a going round." People like to go to see these tough and hardy men as they try for prizes at such contests as bareback bronc riding, saddle bronc riding, bull riding, calf roping, steer roping, and bulldogging.

How would *You* like to be one of the cowboys in these photographs? How do you suppose this bareback rider feels on top of this bucking bronc? How many hands does he use to hold on? Do you think he can stay on much longer? How is the horse's back when he is bucking? How are his legs?

Look at this cowboy in the middle. He's a saddle bronc rider, and he's about ready to hit the dust. Do you suppose it hurts very much when he falls? How long do you think he stayed on the horse before he flew off? Do you think the horse's hoofs might come down hard when he bucks? Would you rather ride a bronc with or without a saddle?

How about this bull rider? Look at those horns. Do you suppose the bull is very happy about having a man on his back? Do you suppose the crowds are cheering for the cowboy to stay on? Is the grandstand full of people? Do you think it must be very dusty there? Why?

Did you ever play with a lasso? Can you show us how a cowboy swings one? See how close the cowboy is to the calf. Do you think the loop will go around the calf's neck? What happens if it does? Did you ever see the cowboy jump off his horse and try to throw the calf down and tie its legs together while the horse pulls back to keep the rope taut? He must do it very, very fast in order to win the prize? How heavy do you think this calf is in the corner? Do you think the cowboy must be very strong to lift him?

How are the cowboys dressed? What is on their feet? Do they wear spurs? What are chaps? What is on their heads? What is the fence for?

Which do you think is the most exciting part of a rodeo? Make a picture about it.

Photo Credit: Rodeo Photographer, Frank Milne

Photo Credit: Rodeo Photographer, Frank Milne

Photo Credit: Robert Ulmer

HOUSE ON PAMET RIVER, Edward Hopper
Courtesy of: Collection of Whitney Museum of American Art, New York

Photograph Collection

GREAT BIG HOUSES

How would you like to live in a huge house? Can you think of the largest house you have ever seen? Was it a two-story house? Did you ever see a house with a high pointed roof? Or one with many peaks and even towers? How many chimneys would you like your house to have? Think of how many doors you would need and how many windows. Some windows have many panes. Look at the different shapes of windows on these pictures. Some are rounded on the top. Can you find a diamond shaped window? A round one? One that is curved on the top? What are shutters for? Would you like to live in a house with a frilly balcony? What about the pillars on the porches of some of these houses? Would you like to have steps going up to the door with railings on each side? Would your house be made of bricks, wood, rock, plaster? What sort of front door would you like? A double door? What color would it be? What kind of texture would your roof have? What if you lived in a scarey-looking house? Which of these houses looks the happiest? Do any of them look lonely as if they needed a family to come and paint them and love them? What color would you paint your house? Would you like to have a fence around it? Would you like trees, flowers, and bushes around your house?

City houses are sometimes squeezed tightly together. They need to have a fire escape? Some houses sit on top of a garage.

Paint a picture of a large house that you would like to live in.

Photo Credit: Robert Ulmer

Photo Credit: Robert Ulmer

Photo Credit: Robert Ulmer

Photo Credit: John E. Schrader

Photo Credit: Jon Else

THE BROOKLYN BRIDGE: VARIATION ON AN OLD THEME, Joseph Stella
Courtesy of: Collection of Whitney Museum of American Art, New York

Photograph Collection
BRIDGES: OVER AND UNDER

Many grown-up artists as well as children have enjoyed painting pictures about bridges near their homes. What bridges have you crossed?

Bridges are of many types. The first bridges men made were probably of logs and ropes. Today, engineers design long suspension bridges, drawbridges, arch bridges, cantilever bridges, vertical lifts, continuous spans, arcade bridges, and even foot bridges in parks. Some of these bridges are very, very long, and some stand high over rivers or canyons. They all must be strong enough to support heavy traffic and to endure terrible storms.

What are some of the things that cross over bridges? . . . . Trains, people, cars, buses, trucks, motorcycles.

What are some of the things under bridges? . . . . Big ships, little boats, fish, rivers, bays, canyons, river banks with trees and rocks, fishermen, reflections.

How are the shapes of the bridges in these photographs different from each other? What materials were used in making them? What colors are bridges painted? Did you ever see a bridge raise and lower to let ships pass under it? Can you find diamond and triangle shapes in the construction of any of these bridges? Can you see any rivets holding the metal together? Can you find the photograph of a bridge that is supported with arches? Can you see the long steel cables forming a long graceful curve from tower to tower? When you crossed a bridge such as this, did you bend your head back to see the tops of the towers? Were they as tall as a tall building? Could you see over the railings on the sides as you drove along? Did your car make any noise when you drove across?

Did you ever cross a bridge at night when it was sparkling with lights? Did you ever cross a bridge in a rain or snow storm or when it was covered with fog?

Draw a bridge that you know about.

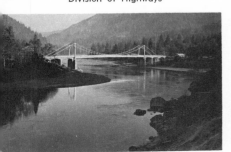

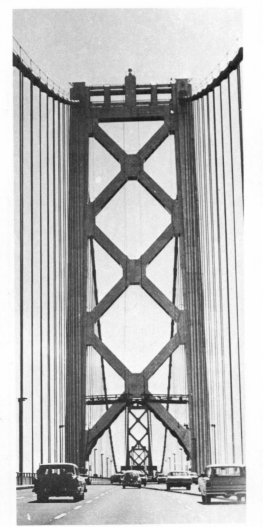

SUNDAY AFTERNOON ON THE ISLAND OF LA GRANDE JATTE, Georges Seurat
Courtesy of: The Art Institute of Chicago
Helen Birch Bartlett memorial collection

35 mm. Slide Collections

A 35 millimeter camera enables a teacher to create his own collection of colored slides on any subject he desires. All the aspects of family trips, community events, and all sorts of people, plants, animals, and things can be grouped and brought into the classroom via the projected image.

Vivid colors, stopped motions, enlarged details, and unusual viewpoints are isolated and framed on the screen for concentrated viewing on the part of the children. Showing numerous varieties of one thing widens the scope of the child's world, the verbal interchange of which centers on the child's experiences in relation to that subject. This technique will review experiences and can enrich a child's thoughts on the subject.

35 mm. Slide Collection
AT THE BEACH

What kind of beach have you visited? Was it near a lake, a river, or an ocean? Did you walk or go in a car or bus? What did you see when you first arrived at the beach? These slides show people sunbathing on the sand, in beach chairs, under umbrellas, and on blankets. Do you see the life guard? Where is he sitting? Were there any motorboats or sailboats when you went to the beach? Was anyone fishing? Did you see seagulls? Perhaps a group of beach boys was playing guitars. Some days, the beach is warm, and sometimes we need to wear a sweater or jacket. Were there trees near your beach?

Have you done any of the things these children are doing at the beach? They have rubber rafts, beach boards, and inner tubes. How does it feel to lie down and let the waves wash up on your legs? Do you have to wash off the sand that sticks to your skin? This boy is taking his dog for a swim.

Children like to dig in the sand and build things. Some make sand castles, roads, tunnels, or just plain holes so they can watch the water come up. Can you pack dry sand as you do wet sand? Bits of shells, rocks, pebbles, and wood make fine walls and fences. What else can you build with things you find at the beach? Do you like to have your father help you? Amy and Eric have made a fine horse from drift wood. Their sister Heidi helped them design monsters from seaweed and wood.

Was the sand warm on your bare feet? Did the water feel cold? Was the sand wet or dry? Is wet sand a different color from dry sand? Do you like to play beachcomber and discover things? What are some of the things you have found on the sand and in the shallow water? Do you remember their shapes, colors, textures? Did any of the creatures you found smell of the beach? Was the wind blowing? Did you carry a bucket for your treasures? Who was with you? Was there a surf? What sort of noise did it make? Did you get sunburned?

SUGGESTED TOPICS for DRAWING, PAINTING and MODELING
    Walking on the beach
    Building on the beach
    We are beachcombing
    Playing in the water at the beach
    Watching fishermen at the beach
    Sunbathing at the beach
    Swimming with my dog at the beach

35 mm. Slide Collection

TREES

Trees are like people . . some are fat; some are thin. Some are graceful and delicate, some are strong and sturdy. Some seem angry, greedy, friendly, tired, happy. Some are tender and young. Some are gnarled and old.

CHESTNUT TREES AT JAS DE BOUFFAN, Paul Cezanne
Courtesy of: The Minneapolis Institute of Arts
The William Hood Dunwoody Fund

Trees may be felled by wind or by axe. Trees seem to be marching in orchard rows. Some trees are grabbing at the sky. Wet boughs may be broken by tossing winds. There are sharp pointed branches, twisted twigs. There are roots exposed and weathered. Trunks are bent by strong coastal winds and timber line gales.

Tiny buds, pink and white blossoms in spring fall and cover the ground beneath. Some trees are heavy with fruit in summer and fall. Some trees are bare and stark in winter, holding heavy mounds of snow.

There is rough bark, smooth bark, bark that is shiny and light.

Some trees have knotholes and needles, pointed leaves, and round leaves.

A roost, a nest, a concert hall for birds, these are provided by trees.

Can you stand like a tree and bend in the wind? Can you *Feel* like a tree in summer rain? Can your fingers hold a nest? Can a squirrel run up your trunk? What kind of tree would you choose to be?

Make a picture about that kind of tree.

35 mm. Slide Collection
CHOOSING OUR CHRISTMAS TREE

Did you go with your family to buy your Christmas tree? Did you go in the mountains and cut your own tree? Or did you buy it in a special Christmas tree lot? Do you remember the wonderful, sharp smell of Christmas trees? Were there a great many from which to make your selection? What colors of trees did you see? How tall were they? Could you touch the top of the tallest one? And were you taller than some of the small ones?

How did the Christmas trees stand up? What were the needles on the branches like? Did you touch them? Did they prick your fingers a little?

How did you take your tree home? Who went with you? How were you dressed?

Draw a picture about choosing your family's Christmas tree.

Divergent Paths . . . Related Topics for . . .

ROUNDABOUT HAPPENINGS

Films, Film Strips and 8 mm. Film Loops

Billy's Helicopter Ride, Coronet; Boats and Ships, EBJ; Boy of Mexico: Juan and His Donkey, Coronet; Boyhood of Abraham Lincoln, Coronet; Old Woman and Her Pig, McGraw Hill; Owl and the Pussy Cat, Halas and Batchela Sterling; Zoo Babies, Coronet; Baby Animals, McGraw Hill; Squeak the Squirrel, Churchill; Wonders in Your Own Backyard, Churchill; African Fauna, Hoefler Productions; World of Little Things, Moody Institute of Science; Sparky, the Colt, Coronet; Birds of the Inland Waterways, Coronet; Prickly, the Porcupine, Coronet; Secrets of the Underwater World, Disney

Books

The Circus, Ideals Pub. Co., Van B. Hopper, editor
Circus! by editors of Country Beautiful magazine, Hawthorn Books
A House for Everyone, Betty Miles, Alfred A. Knopf
Dinosaurs and Other Prehistoric Animals, Carlene Geis, Grosset & Dunlap
The Strange World of Dinosaurs, John H. Ostrom, GP Putnam's Sons
The Big Book of Real Helicopters, Clayton Knight, Grosset & Dunlap How and Why
    Series, Wonder Books
The Sea and Its Wonderful Creatures, Ronald Rood, Whitman Pub. Co.
Flowers and What They Are, Mary Elting, Whitman Pub. Co.
The Beginning Knowledge Book of Bees and Wasps, Jay Heavilin, Macmillan Co.
Ships, Paul Hamlyn, London
Living Mammals of the World, Ivan T. Sanderson, Hanover House
Pictorial Encyclopedia of the Animal Kingdom, V. J. Stanek, Crown Pub. Inc.

Poems

One Thousand Poems for Children, Elizabeth H. Sechrist, Macrae Smith Co.
The First Book of Poetry, selected by Isabel J. Peterson, Franklin Watts, Inc.
The Birds and the Beasts Were There, selected by Wm. Cole, World Pub. Co.
Everybody Ought to Know, selected by Ogden Nash, J. B. Lippincott Co.

People I'd Like to Keep, Mary O'Neill, Doubleday and Co.

The Big Golden Book of Poetry, edited by Jane Werner, Golden Press

I Met a Man, John Ciardi, Houghton Mifflin Co.

Cats and Bats and Things with Wings, Conrad Aiken, Atheneum

Read Me a Poem, chosen by Ellen L. Buell, Grosset & Dunlap

Nibble Nibble Poems for Children, Margaret Wise Brown, Young Scott Books

The Golden Treasury of Poetry, selected by Louis Untermeyer

Favorite Poems Old and New, selected by Helen Ferris, Doubleday and Co.

Poems to Grow On, Compiled by Jean McKee Thompson, Beacon Press

Prefabulous Animiles, James Reeves, E. P. Dutton

Stuff and Nonsense, Edgar Parker, Pantheon

The Poetry-Drawing Book, edited by Wm. Cole and Julia Colmore, Simon and Schuster

The Second Poetry-Drawing Book, edited by Wm. Cole and Julia Colmore, Simon and Schuster

I Go Out, Muriel Rukeyser, Harper

I Wonder How I Wonder Why, Aileen Fisher, Abelard-Schuman

Records

"Journey to the Moon," LP 158, Golden Record

"Just So Stories," by Rudyard Kipling, 823 Vol. 1 and 124, Vol. 2, Spoken Arts, Inc.

Prokofiev: "Peter and the Wolf," Tchaikovsky: "Nutcracker Suite," Leonard Bernstein, NY Philharmonic, Columbia Masterworks

"With Young People in Mind," Richard Dyer-Bennet, Dyer-Bennet Records

"Animals, Funny Folk and Wee People," Gateway Recordings, Inc.

"The Pied Piper and the Hunting of the Snark," read by Boris Karloff, Caedmon T1075

"A Child's Introduction to the American Indian," Prestige International 13076

"Folk Songs for Little Sailors," Riverside Wonderland 1424

"Grimm's Fairy Tales" — The Hanky Pank Players, RCA Camden, CAL 1037

"Dr. Seuss Presents: If I Ran the Zoo and Dr. Seuss' Sleep Book," RCA Camden

"Jack and the Beanstalk," Shari Lewis, RCA Camden, Cal 1052

"The Lollipop Tree," Burl Ives, Harmony-Columbia

"Galloping on My Dinosaur and other Fun Songs for Children," Larry Thor, Harmony Columbia

"Holiday Fun for Children," Harmony Columbia HL 9531

"A Trip to Magic Animal Land," Harmony Columbia HL 9541

"Children's Songs for a Rainy Day," Harmony Columbia, HL 9524

"Authentic Calliope Music," Major Records Vol. 1 Monaural 1001

"Screamers — Circus Marches," Mercury Records

"Famous Pirate Stories" — William Bendix, Cricket Records, CR 30

"Let's Fly to the Moon," Playtime Records

"Let's Build a House," Vocalion, Decca

"Let's Go to the Farm," Vocalion, Decca

"Let's Visit the Forests," Vocalion, Decca

"Stories and Songs about America's Pioneers," Vocalion, Decca

"Stories and Songs about the Sea," Vocalion, Decca

"All about Wheels and Wings," Vocalion, Decca

"The Adventures of Little Orley," Vocalion, Decca

"March Along," Stirring Marches for Children, Wonderland

"Raggedy Ann — Songs and Stories," Vocalion, Decca

"Patrick Muldoon and his Magic Balloon," RCA Camden

"Holidays," told and sung by Tom Glazer, RCA Victor
LY 101

"Grimm's Fairy Tales," Danny Kaye, Golden LP 92

"Birds, Beasts, Bugs and Little Fishes," Animal Folk Songs,
Pete Seeger, Folkways Records, FC 7010

"Let's Listen Stories," Julie Harris and Boris Karloff, Caedmon TC 1182

"Noisy and Quiet, Big and Little," told and sung by Tom
Glazer, RCA Camden, Cal 1070

"The Silly Record," by Stoo Hample, Harmony Columbia,
HL 9536

"The Magic World of Circuses and Clowns," with Robert
Q. Lewis, MGM

Photograph Collections

Things the wind does; City buildings; Cars, trucks, and
buses; Ranch life; Inside caves; Living on an island;
Flowers

35 mm. Slide Collections

Decorating our Christmas tree; Opening gifts on Christmas
morning; Helping in the Garden; Washing the car;
Teaching my dog a trick; Fish Hatchery; National Parks;
Family Picnic; Camping Trip; Our Fishing trip

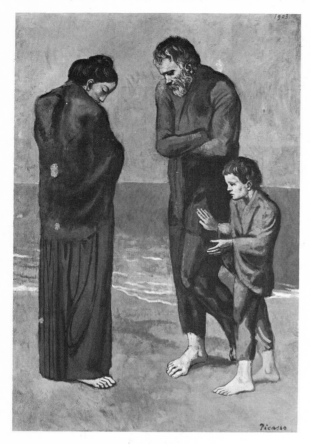

THE TRAGEDY, Pablo Picasso
Courtesy of: National Gallery of Art, Washington, D.C.
Chester Dale Collection

Imagination Stretchers...
Reaching Beyond the Self

Stretch — reach out, extend, draw out, expand, spread, promote, hoist, lift, boost, pull

All of the motivations in this category emphasize the *extensive* use of the imagination. They stress inventiveness, creativeness, dream-like thinking, improvisation, flights of fancy, humor, exploration, unreal objects, strong feelings, and empathetic attitudes.

A child's imaginative powers can be definitely given a boost by encouraging him to think about odd configurations, unreal situations, unnatural objects, pretend events, strange environments, silly subjects, fantastic and novel ideas, projected feelings and intense emotions. This section will present some examples of motivational dialogues that can be used to stimulate the imagination.

Inciting Intense Emotions . . . Feeling with Depth
Emotion — sensibility, sensation, sentiment, feeling

Both the positive and the negative feelings of love, sorrow, fear, hate, regret, joy, longing, disgust, anger, surprise, pride, amusement, pain, and thankfulness provide a common world of expression for young children. Inner chaos can become ordered and somewhat understood if these feelings are articulated in art forms. In a curriculum stressing a constant barrage of intellectual stimuli, the strong emotional feelings of children often become buried or distorted and unrelated. Art provides an outlet where they may find expression. Permitting the child to use his imagination and encouraging him to do so at the early level of education can be of benefit for him in self-expression in all areas of his studies in school and in his work in adulthood.

Inciting Intense Emotions

I Love Our Baby

Do you have a baby brother or a baby sister? Do you ever hold him or hug him or kiss him? Is he soft? Does he have much hair? Can you make him smile? How many teeth does he have? What toys does he like to play with? Do you ever shake his rattle or squeeze a squeaky toy to make him laugh? Where does your baby like to play — in a jump seat or in a play pen? Are you ever allowed to feed him with a spoon or hold his bottle? Do you hand him his toys when he drops them from his high chair? Taking care of a baby, helping him, and talking to him is a good way to show him that we love him. Loving makes us want to share all the things we like with him. How do you show your baby that you love him?

Draw a picture about yourself and your baby brother or sister.

"AFFECTION", William Zorach
Courtesy of: Munson-Williams-Proctor
Institute Collection
Utica, New York

Inciting Intense Emotions

MY PET

Fur, feather, scales, hair, shell . . . which does *your* pet have?

What do you do with your pet? How do you play with it? Can you hold your pet in your hands? Or is he too big for you to put your arms around? Do you like to pet him?

What color is your pet? What shape is his body? Are his ears long or short, soft, pointed, floppy? Does his nose quiver? Does he have whiskers? What kind of feet does he have? Who has a pet with a long tail? A stubby tail? Whose pet can swim? What kind of home does your pet have? Is it a house, a cage, a pen, or a bowl?

How do you feed your pet? Did your pet ever have babies? What do you feed him? Will he eat from your hand? Does he eat from a bowl?

Did your pet ever run away and get lost? Were you sad? When you found him, how did you feel? Does your pet know you and act happy when you return home? Did your pet ever get sick and have to be taken to a veterinarian?

What kind of noise does your pet make? Does he smell? Can you take your pet for a walk?

What if you stepped on your pet? What if *he* stepped on *you*?

Draw, paint, model, or cut out your interpretation of your pet or a pet that you would like to have.

SUGGESTED TOPICS for DRAWING,
   PAINTING, and MODELING
     Walking my pet
     Stroking my pet
     Feeding my pet
     Riding my pet
     Bathing my pet
     My pet sleeping
     My pet and her babies
     When I lost my pet
     My pet running
     The pet I would like to have.

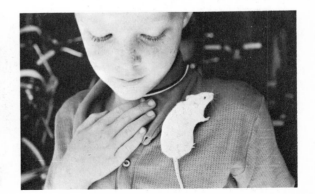

MOTHER AND CHILDREN, Pierre Auguste Renoir
Copyrighted by: The Frick Collection, New York

Inciting Intense Emotions
MY FAVORITE TOY

Which of your toys do you like the most? How long have you had it? Who gave it to you? How do you play with it?

Can you hold your favorite toy, such as a doll; or does it, like a firetruck or tricycle, hold you? Is it soft? Is it a bright color? Is it light or dark? Can you build with it and play pretend things? Is it shiny? Is it hard? Is it rough? Does your favorite toy make any kind of noise, such as crying or ringing? Which is larger, you or your toy? Is it old and worn or brand new?

Draw a picture about you and your favorite toy.

Inciting Intense Emotions

I Stubbed My Toe on the Sidewalk

Do you remember how much your toe hurt the last time you stubbed it while running on the sidewalk? How were you running? Were you chasing someone or running home to supper after your mother called? What did you trip on or fall over? When you fell, did it take you a long time to hit the sidewalk? Did you fall flat on your stomach with your hands stretched out in front of you or did you fall on your knees? Did you skin your nose, knees, hands, or elbows? Did your toe or other parts of your body bleed or get dirty? Did you start crying right away, or didn't you cry at all? Did tears roll down your cheeks? Did your face feel warm? Did you hold your toe and look at it right away? If you did this, were you sitting on the sidewalk? Or did you get up and run home right away? Did your mother or someone else clean your wound and put a bandage on it? Did she hold you until you stopped crying?

Draw a picture of stubbing your toe on the sidewalk. Will you make any part of your body bigger? Can you make the picture fill the whole page? Will you use any different colors to show how it felt?

Inciting Intense Emotions

Getting a Shot at the Doctor's Office

Do you know your doctor's name? What is it? Does your doctor know your name? What does your doctor wear when he is in his office? What is on his head? What is around his neck? Does a nurse help him? How does she dress?

Can you remember going to your doctor to have a check-up? Have you ever been to his office to have a shot? What did the doctor or the nurse use to give you the shot? How big was the needle? What shape was it? Was the shot that you remember one to immunize you against getting sick, or was it an antibiotic to cure an infection?

Did you stand or sit when you had the shot? How did you hold your arm? Were you frightened? Sometimes boys and girls cry a little bit when they have a shot. Did it hurt you very much? Was your arm sore and swollen afterward? How did you hold your arm when you left the office? Did it feel larger than your other arm?

Draw a picture about getting a shot at your doctor's office. Think about how you will arrange the people on your page. Who is taller, you or your doctor? Will you show yourself sitting or standing? Fill the page with your drawing.

Inciting Intense Emotions

SAYING GOODBYE TO GRANDMOTHER

When Grandmother left to go back to her own home, did you: help carry suitcases, see and hear the train rush into the station, see the conductor, watch him punch her ticket, see other people arriving and departing, hear the "all aboard," see the baggage being loaded, kiss her goodbye, feel a few tears come to your eyes, wave as the train pulled away? Did you feel sad and wish she could visit you again very soon? Did the station feel empty when the train was out of sight? Did you think Grandmother felt a little sad, too? Does she live far away? Will you go to see her sometime, too?

Draw a picture about how you felt when your Grandmother (or someone you love) left after a visit at your house. Perhaps your Grandmother left on a plane or bus or car.

Whimsy, Fantasy, Humor . . . Designing Images

Whimsy — curious, odd, peculiar, freakish, waggish, droll, queer, capricious, quaint

Fantasy — bizarre, fanciful, irrational, unreal, absurd, dream-like, castle-building

Humor — caprice, witty, funny, hilarious, jest, joke

Of natural and instant appeal to children are the topics that deal with curious, whimsical, fantastic, or funny ideas. Helping children to grow creatively often means encouraging them to:

Explore new and bizarre ideas
Pretend and make-believe
Manipulate weird visual relationships
Push boundaries beyond the already known barriers
Laugh at silly and absurd situations
Rearrange old ideas into fresh relationships
Experiment with novel thoughts
Solve wild tasks in individual ways

This is an area in which young children will delight and proceed with enthusiasm.

Figure, cow; Dutch——18th Century
Courtesy of: The Metropolitan Museum of Art
Gift of Henry G. Marquand, 1894

Whimsy, Fantasy, Humor

THE ANIMAL I WOULD LIKE TO HAVE IN MY BACKYARD

What animal would you like to keep in your back-yard? A kangaroo could put you in his pocket and take you for a ride. What animal could put you in *your* pocket — a mouse, a lizard . . . or *What*?

What animal could you have for a swimming buddy — a penguin, a porpoise, a duck, a frog . . . or *What*?

What animal would help you climb and swing in trees — an opossum, a monkey, a squirrel . . . or *What*?

What animal would protect you? Such a ferocious beast would probably have to be kept locked in a cage or tied up, but you could invite your friends over to help you toss food to him. Would it be a lion, tiger, hyena, skunk . . . or *What*?

What animal would eat the most? Pigs are fat and weighty, but they eat almost anything you offer them. Does any animal have a larger mouth than a hippo? Would you feed him hay, meat, grain, milk . . . or *What*?

What animal would be the noisiest? An owl would make night-time noises if you kept him in the tree outside your window. What kind of noise would your pet make? A roar, a peep, a bark, a whinny . . . or *What*?

Make or model the animal you would like to have in your backyard.

Whimsy, Fantasy, Humor

INSIDE ME . . . WHAT I THINK I LOOK LIKE INSIDE

Can you feel your heart beat? Where is your heart? Do you know that your heart is like a pump pumping blood all over your body? Did you ever cut yourself and bleed? Blood vessels carry the blood that the heart pumps.

Take a deep breath. Where did the air go when you breathed it in? Lungs are a little bit like balloons in that they can take air in and let it out. What do you suppose protects your lungs? Let's feel our rib cage.

What else do you suppose is inside you? There are the stomach, liver, kidneys, intestines, and many other organs that work together to keep you healthy.

Your skin and flesh are soft. Could you stand up if you had no bones? Let's feel our shins. Let's feel our arm bones and our knuckles and all the bones in our fingers. Why do you need a kneecap? Why do you have elbows? Can you twist your feet around and find your ankle bones? Where are your brains? What do you suppose your backbone looks like?

Doctors, of course, know exactly what our bodies are like inside, but we can *imagine*. Use your "X-ray vision" and draw a picture of what you think you look like inside.

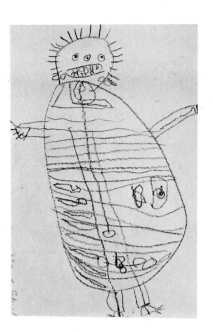

Whimsy, Fantasy, Humor

IMAGINARY BIRDS

If you could be an imaginary bird for a day, how would you want to look and what kind of personality would you want to have? Would you be a dignified or a conceited bird? A bird of prey or a sweet little chirper? A magnificent, kingly bird? A cruel, hungry bird? Or a graceful, delicate bird?

What sort of tail might this imaginary bird have? Will you make it sticking up straight, or spreading out, or drooping on the ground? Will your bird have a long body or a fat one? Some birds have long necks and some have short ones. How will your bird's head be shaped? Will he have a topknot? How are his eyes shaped? What color are they?

What about the wings? Will you make them outspread as if in flight or tucked down by his side? Will the bird's feathers be small and overlap? Will you choose many colors for the feathers? What position are the bird's legs in? Where will they be if he is flying?

Will your bird be pecking angrily at another bird or yanking a juicy worm out of the garden, or will you have him chirping gaily on a branch? What might be near him? Will he be perched in a nest high in a tree or on a cliff, or will he be flying with other birds? What time of day is it? Choose a dark color of paper for your background if it is a night time bird. Will you show a stormy sky?

If you are working with cut and torn paper, make the larger parts first and keep adding details with more bits and pieces of paper. Keep your fingers close together when you are tearing shapes. You might crumple and crease some of the pieces to make a variety of textures.

Make (or model) an imaginary bird and show what he is doing. He need not look like any real bird that you have ever seen.

Whimsy, Fantasy, Humor

WITCHES MAKING BREW

3 teaspoons powdered bat wing
4 cups of black cat fur
3/4 cup dust from a haunted belfry
3 ghosts' eyeballs

Bring to a boil in a big black kettle and stir with two feathers from the tail of an owl.

What do you suppose this recipe is for? Who would use it? It's the time of year when witches are dusting off their cookbooks and stirring up potions and brews of all sorts. Have you seen any witches lately?

Do you suppose the witches are getting their brooms ready to ride on Halloween night? They will probably gather in some dark and damp cave and exchange recipes and may even try out a few new ones.

How do witches dress? How tall are they? Do you suppose some of the younger witches might be small and some of the older witches fat? What do they wear on their heads? What sort of hair do they have? Is it long or short? Do you think a witch *ever* combs her hair? What sort of hands does a witch have? How are the sleeves of her dress? Do you imagine that her cape billows out as she swoops across the sky on her broom? Would you like to have a nose like a witch? Is a witch's face wrinkled? What sort of ears does she have? What does she wear on her feet?

How large do you suppose a witch's kettle might be? How many witches can you draw around the kettle? How many will be helping to stir the brew? Will steam and awful smells be coming out of the kettle? Will you show some witches arriving on their broom sticks with cats riding behind? Will the moon be full or crescent-shaped? Will there be owls or bats and scratchy, scarey trees around the kettle?

Make a painting about witches making brew on Halloween night.

Whimsy, Fantasy, Humor

MAGIC FLOWERS

Real flowers grow slowly. Magic flowers can sprout and bud and open as fast as your brush or crayons or scissors can move. Real flowers make seeds which almost *seems* like magic. But what things can you think of that magic flowers could make and do? Real flowers have roots beneath the ground that gather water and food. What do you suppose magic flowers might do with their roots? What color of pollen could magic flowers have? Could the pollen shoot through the air like fireworks? Could the tendrils be swings for imaginary elves? What kind of butterflies or birds could flutter near such magic flowers? Could magic flowers walk or dance? Could small doves hide in the cup-like blossoms? What if lemonade were in the stalk of your magic flower? What if the leaves changed colors when they were touched? What shape of petals might magic flowers have? What if they turned to candy when you picked them? Could magic flowers shoot popcorn? Could your magic flowers create their own raindrops? Could they make music in some manner? Could you design a flower that was decorated with magic colored lights? Would your flower wear a crown or have wings?

Make a cut paper picture, a painting, or a drawing of your ideas for a number of different kinds of magic flowers.

Whimsy, Fantasy, Humor

A Christmas Angel

How tall will you design your Christmas angel? What kind of hair will it have — long, short, curly, straight, braided, blonde, brunette, or auburn? Will it be graceful? Will it have a beautifully curving neck? Will it be smiling, singing, blowing a horn, or playing a flute? What will it be carrying? What kind of clothing will your angel wear? What will it have on its feet? Will it be flying? Sitting? Standing? Lying down? How will you show the texture of the wings? What color will they be? How will the wings be shaped? Would you like to talk to your angel? Would you like to pretend you are an angel? How do you think it would feel to have wings and halo?

Draw a picture of what you think a lovely Christmas angel might look like, or you may model one with clay.

TEACHER'S NOTE:

In addition to the regular painting or cutting and pasting materials, try these imagination stimulators:
1. Gold and silver paint
2. Gold and silver paper

THE POSTMAN ROULIN, Vincent van Gogh
Courtesy of: Museum of Fine Arts, Boston
Gift of Robert Treat Paine II

If I Were . . . . Identifying with People and Things

Identifying — empathizing, coinciding, treating as the same, feeling as

First glimmerings of social awareness can be sparked by art motivations that call for the child to project his thoughts, feelings, and perceptions into another person or object. In these motivations, the child is required to place himself in another person's or object's position and imagine how he would feel, what he would see, and what he would think and do.

The child may be expected to delve for some factual information and penetrate into the details of the other person's or object's being before he will be able to identify himself with the person or object with which he is dealing. He can do this through the use of photographs, films, books, stories, poems, or by direct contact with the subject. This technique should be fun for children and teacher alike because children occasionally enjoy games of pretend.

If I Were . . .

IF I WERE A POSTMAN

Does your postman walk along your street or ride in a small car? How does he carry the letters and magazines and small packages? What does he wear? Where does he leave the mail at your house? Is your mailbox on the house or is it a box along the street? Do you suppose the mailman gets tired of walking and carrying a heavy load all day?

Would you like to be a postman when you grow up? A famous artist named Vincent van Gogh painted this portrait of a postman many years ago.

Draw or paint how you would look if you were a postman.

If I Were . . .

IF I WERE A BALLOON MAN

Did you ever see a balloon man? Did you ever buy a balloon from him? Did you ever let go of the string on your balloon and watch it vanish in the distant sky?

What colors are balloons? How many shapes of balloons have you seen? How many balloons can a balloon man hold? About how large is one of the balloons.

Are the balloons on strings pulling above his head, or are they on sticks? Does he need to hold them in both hands or just in one hand? Where does he put the money when someone pays him? What kind of clothing does he wear?

How do you suppose it would feel to be a balloon man and hold a huge cluster of bright balloons? Do you think your arm might get tired? How would you like to look up over your head and see as many as fifty balloons?

Cut out, paint, or draw yourself as a balloon man.

If I Were . . .

IF I WERE A GRASSHOPPER

Did you ever catch a grasshopper? How do you suppose the grasshopper felt when you caught him? Do you suppose you looked like a giant to him? How do grasshoppers move around besides hopping? (Walking, flying) What would you eat if you were a grasshopper? Where do you suppose you would go to find the best soft green food? Would you look for a place where leaves would offer you protection from birds and small boys looking for fish bait? Did you know that grasshoppers are musicians? They rub their legs and wings together to make music. A grasshopper is never a caterpillar. It looks like a grown-up grasshopper when it hatches from its egg, but it must shed its skin several times before it has wings. How do you suppose it feels to shed your skin and discover that you have grown wings?

See the fishbone design on the large hind legs. He has three pairs of legs and it's a good thing he goes barefoot. Think of tying six pairs of shoe strings every morning! What kind of feet must a grasshopper have to enable him to climb straight up the stalk of a plant?

What color are grasshoppers? Are their bodies soft or hard? Why do you suppose his eyes are so large? Would you like to have a pair of antennae fastened to your head? Look at the heavy "collar." It is almost like a suit of armor on his shoulders. When a grasshopper's wings are spread out, they are beautiful colors — red, yellow, and green. He keeps them tucked on his back when they are not in use. His abdomen is made up of many parts. What shape is it? What shape is his head?

Let's *be* grasshoppers crawling along a juicy leaf in the garden. You will have to lie flat on the floor and bend your elbows and pretend that they are the grasshopper's hind legs. The other two pairs of legs will have

to be imagined. Keep your feet together and pretend that they are the long narrow body. Wiggle your antennae!

If you were a grasshopper, where would you be, what would you do, and how would you look? Draw it.

Photo Credit: Bob Taylor

Courtesy of: Textron's Bell Helicopter Co.

Courtesy of: New York Airways Inc.

If I Were . . .

IF I WERE A HELICOPTER PILOT

Who has seen a helicopter? Was it on the ground or in the sky? Has anyone actually *Ridden* in a helicopter? Would you like to ride in one someday? What insect is a helicopter like? What can a helicopter do that an airplane can't? What are some of the important jobs that helicopters do? Do you know some of the things that helicopters can do? They can:

> Help round up horses and cattle on ranches
> Rescue people with long ropes from the ocean or high cliffs or in jungles
> Land on tops of skyscrapers
> Taxi people from downtown to the airport
> Help build power towers by lifting materials to the top
> Help construct churches and other tall buildings
> Help control brush and forest fires
> Spray insecticides on crops to kill pests
> Help the Army, Navy, Air Force, and Marines
> Patrol traffic and help policemen

What is the shape of a helicopter? What is on top of it? How many people can ride in one? Do helicopters have wheels, or what do they use for landing? How

Courtesy of: Bell Helicopter Co.
Fort Worth, Texas

Courtesy of: Bell Helicopter Co.
Fort Worth, Texas

does the pilot see out? What is on the helicopter's tail? Can it land on water? How?

Which kind of helicopter would you like to ride in? What sort of job would you like to do? What would you see below you while in a helicopter? Do you suppose it would be noisy? Would there be any emblems or words or letters painted on the sides of your helicopter?

If you could be any kind of helicopter pilot you wished, which would you be? Draw or paint or cut out a picture about what you would be doing.

Courtesy of: Bell Helicopter Co.
Fort Worth, Texas

Courtesy of: Pacific Gas and Electric Company

Courtesy of: Bell Helicopter Co.
Fort Worth, Texas

Courtesy of: Copy Photograph, Bell Helicopter Company
Photo Credit: Wide World

Courtesy of: Textron's Bell Helicopter Co.

Photo Credit: George Nicks

Photo Credit: George Nicks

Photo Credit: George Nicks

Photo Credit: George Nicks

Photo Credit: George Nicks

If I Were . . .

If I Were a Sky Diver

Did you ever dive off a board into a swimming pool or jump down from the limb of a tree? How do you think it would feel to jump from the door of an airplane high, high above the ground and fall and spin rapidly through space before you yanked the cord of your parachute? Men who do this are called sky divers. Would you like to be one someday?

How do you think these brave men must dress? What do they wear on their feet to protect their ankles when they land on the hard ground? What do they wear on their heads to protect their skulls? Where do they carry their parachute? How do you think a sky diver gauges how high up he is? How does he know how long to wait before he pulls the cord? What would he see below him as he falls through the sky? What would he see if he looked above him? Around him?

Sky divers usually ride in a propellor plane with a single wing and a door that opens wide for easy jumping. Some sky divers dive with a friend or two along. How many wheels are on the plane? How is the tail shaped? Do you suppose the sky diver falls rapidly when he jumps out? What position is his body in when he is falling? What is the shape of his parachute when it is open? How does he control the chute and make it go where he wants it to go? Do you suppose the wind whistles through his chute strings? How would it feel to hit the ground and then quickly manipulate your chute strings so the wind wouldn't blow you away? What if you landed in a lake or an ocean?

If you were a sky diver, what part of the expedition would be the most fun? Make a picture about it. What colors will you choose for the airplane, for your diving outfit, and for the parachute?

Photo Credit: Frank Binford

Photo Credit: Frank Binford

Photo Credit: Frank Binford

Photo Credit: George Nicks

Photo Credit: George Nicks

If I Were . . .

If I Were a Scarecrow

How long do you suppose you could stand up and hold your arms out straight without getting tired if you were a scarecrow? Can you imagine how it would feel to be a scratchy-looking, old scarecrow and stand in a field of corn or in someone's garden day after day and hold your arms out straight and stiff? Could you really move your arms and legs if you were a scarecrow?

Do you suppose a scarecrow feels that he has an important job? What *is* his job, and how did he get his name? Do you suppose a scarecrow thinks of birds as being friendly?

How would you dress if you were a scarecrow? With what would your body be stuffed? Would your clothes be all new, or would they be old and shabby? What kind of hat would you have? Would you prefer a plaid shirt or a striped one? What color would your overalls or trousers be? What would you have on your feet? Would the sun feel hot on your head? How would it feel to have to stand through every rainstorm and get soaking wet? Do scarecrows make noises? Would you be very angry if crows roosted on your head and shoulders? Would you be cranky or would you be a happy scarecrow? Would you be taller than the corn or the crop you were guarding?

If you were a scarecrow, how would you feel? How would you look? What kind of field or garden would you live in? Use your paper in the vertical position. Show yourself as a scarecrow.

Divergent Paths . . . Related Topics for . . .

IMAGINATION STRETCHERS

Inciting Intense Emotions

I cut my finger; When I helped someone; A scarey day; The saddest think I know; When I said I was sorry; Someone I don't like; An unfair thing; A fight between two animals; When I was very angry; When I tore my new clothes; What I am most thankful for; The funniest thing I ever saw; Visiting my favorite uncle; When Father and I surprised Mother; When I found my lost dog; The happiest day of my life

Whimsy, Fantasy, Humor

What I think a television set looks like inside; What I think a clock looks like inside; What I think my dog looks like inside; What a car looks like inside? The Tooth Fairy; A Snicklehooferlob; A horse swallowed a bouquet of flowers; Wearing a hat full of birds; A dizzy world; Trees that chase squirrels

If I Were

If I were a policeman, nurse, doctor, milkman, skin diver, mechanical man, lizard, butterfly, bumblebee

FRIEZE OF DANCERS, Hilaire Germain Edgar Degas
Courtesy of: The Cleveland Museum of Art
Gift of Hanna Fund

Point of View Changers...
Breaking the Size and Shape Barriers

Change — alter, diversify, modify, innovate, deviate, transform, displace, vary, shift, revamp

In order to maintain and increase flexibility in the young child's emotions and thoughts, this group of motivations suggests to the child a different point of view.

The base line concept whereby the child places all the objects in his picture on a horizontal line on the lower half of the paper can easily become a stereotyped and meaningless vehicle for expression if the child is never encouraged to deviate from it. In these motivations, the child may feel the need to raise the base line to a location near the top of the page if the important ideas are taking place below it. The motivation may induce the child to bend the base line. Multiple base lines may be required to express what the child feels, or the topic may eliminate the need for a base line in preference for another space symbol. When the child draws X-ray pictures, he is presenting a valid point of view in which the interior of something is of more significance than the exterior.

Changing the size and shape of the drawing surface will very frequently spur the child's imaginative concepts and should result in a rich aesthetic product that demonstrates the child's increased ability to relate, clarify, and unify his art forms.

The fluent and flexible child is more likely to be able to deviate from his usual base line concept and from the size and shape of drawing surface which he is accustomed to using while the more rigid child will, at first, be unable to change his stereotyped responses. By assuring such children that their ideas are acceptable and that unusual and untypical expressions are greeted with enthusiasm, the child will feel free to break through his barriers and will achieve a greater flexibility.

Long Horizontal Strip of Paper
A FAMILY OF TIGHTROPE WALKERS

Did you ever try to walk on the curb or on a log that is bridging a stream or just on a line in the sidewalk? Perhaps this is the way circus tightrope walkers start to learn their trade. (Draw a line about eight feet long on the floor with chalk or have a cord or thin rope and lay it on the floor.) Who can be a tightrope walker today? Come and show us how you do it. See how gingerly he puts one foot in front of the other. How long are his steps? How does he keep his balance? What does he do with his arms? How would it feel to be fifty feet or so above the hard ground? Sometimes the tightrope walkers have a net below to break their fall if they slip. Some tightrope walkers use a long pole to help them keep their balance or some use an umbrella so they won't teeter and wobble so much. Do you think a tightrope walker stands straight or bends over? How would you climb up to the tightrope? How would you get down? How would you dress? What would you have on your feet? How would it feel to lose your balance and start to fall? Where would you keep your eyes? Would you move fast or slowly? How would the people look when you were up so high?

An entire family sometimes performs on the high wires. One may ride a bicycle while others use a uni-cycle and the rest walk. What sort of costumes would they be wearing? Draw a family of tightrope walkers on your long, narrow paper. Make the rope extend from one side of your paper to the other.

Long Horizontal Strip of Paper
(Suggested paper dimensions — 6 x 18 or 9 x 24 inches)
A PARADE

When we watch a parade, we see . . .
. . . things that roll:
  Wagons
  Cars
  Trucks
  Bicycles
  Motorcycles
When we watch a parade, we see . . .
. . . things that walk:
  Bands
  Baton twirlers
  Horses
  Drill teams
  Color bearers
  Clowns
  Dogs
When we watch a parade, we hear . . .
. . . exciting sounds:
  Drummers
  Motorcycles
  Bands playing march music
  Sirens
  Horse hoofs
  Marching feet
  Whistles
  Applause
When we watch a parade, we feel . . .
. . . like keeping time with our feet:
  Clapping
  Shouting
  Waving
  Saluting the flag

When we watch a parade, we see . . .
. . . colors:
   Fancy saddles, bridles
   Uniforms
   Shiny French horns
   Bright flags waving
   Sweating horses
   Feathers on band members' hats
   Balloon men
   Dazzling floats and pretty girls
When we watch a parade, we see . . .
. . . a long, long, long line going
   past in front of us down the long, long
   street.
Draw a parade on your long, long paper.

Courtesy of: Jos. Schlitz Brewing Co.

Long Horizontal Strip of Paper

CARS (OR TRAINS) GOING THROUGH A LONG, LONG TUNNEL

Did you ever go through a long tunnel in a car or in a train? Why are tunnels built? Some are very, very long and are cut through hard mountains of rock, and some go under rivers and seas. Subways are tunnels under city streets. How did it feel to enter a tunnel? Did you put your car lights on so you could see or was it lighted with artificial lights? How long did it take to reach the other side? Was it lined with concrete or rocks or brick? How is a tunnel different from a cave? Did the other cars line up in front of and behind you as you drove through? Did you meet any other cars coming the other way? Did your car horn sound differently in the tunnel than it does outside? Could you smell exhaust fumes from the cars?

We will pretend that we have X-ray eyes and can see through a tunnel from the outside and draw a long line of cars (or trains) going through a long, long tunnel. Make your tunnel start at one side of the page and end on the other side and show all kinds of cars (or train cars) entering and driving through it.

Courtesy of: Santa Fe Railway

Courtesy of: State of California
Division of Highways

Courtesy of: State of California
Division of Highways

Long Horizontal Strip of Paper
KENNY CATERPILLAR

(This dialogue is based on a motivation suggested by first grade teacher, Lois Cinnamond.)

Kenny Caterpillar lived in dry, brown grass and was just the color of the dry, brown grass. This protected him from the birds who might be hungry for a fat, juicy caterpillar. But Kenny was unhappy. Do you know why?

Kenny would look up at the brightly colored birds flying over his head, and he wished he could be more like them and not be brown all over. He asked his mother if he could be blue like the bluebirds or grey and red and yellow like the waxwing. But his mother told him not to think such thoughts because if he turned blue or orange or some bright color, the birds would surely see him and eat him. Brown was the best color for him, she said, for if he were any other color, he would have to live in a dark, black hole in the ground.

Kenny thought about the things his mother told him. But he still dreamed of having blue and orange stripes on his back or yellow dots on his tummy. And how he would have loved a purple head and red legs and shiny green eyes!

Kenny felt so happy thinking about all the colors that he wanted to be if he lived in the ground that he found a nice hole and crawled into it. Then he closed his eyes and wished and wished and wished and when he opened his eyes he was the brightest, most beautiful caterpillar you ever saw.

What colors do you think Kenny wished he could be? What kind of designs do you suppose were on his back and tummy? What was on his head? Were all his legs the same color? Did he need large, bright eyes to see in his new home?

Draw Kenny, the long, long caterpillar, with your crayons. Make his head at one end of the paper and his tail at the other end. Use the brightest, richest colors you can think of. When you finish, you may brush thin, dark tempera over the background to show that Kenny is in a dark, black hole.

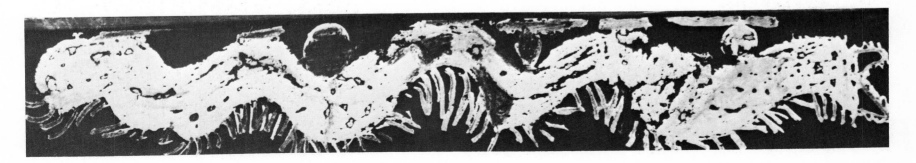

"SNAP THE WHIP," Winslow Homer
Courtesy of: The Butler Institute of American Art
Youngstown, Ohio

Long Horizontal Strip of Paper
PLAYING TUG-OF-WAR

Two teams play tug-of-war and each team has the same number of boys and girls. A line is drawn on the playground, and each team tries to pull the other team over the line.

If we divide our class into two teams, how many will be on each side? Would it be fair to have all girls on one side and all boys on the other?

We start by having each team lined up on either side of the line. Then each person pulls on the rope as hard as he can. How would you hold the rope to keep the best and tightest grip on it? Would you lean backwards as you pulled? How would you place your feet? Would the rope hurt your hands a little? Would you bend your elbows? How would your knees be? Which team will be the winner?

Make a picture about playing tug-of-war on this long, long paper. The two teams will be lined up the entire length of the paper. Each child should be holding the rope and pulling hard.

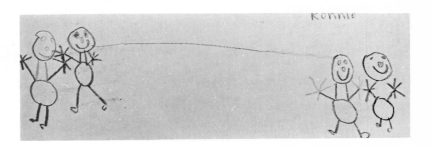

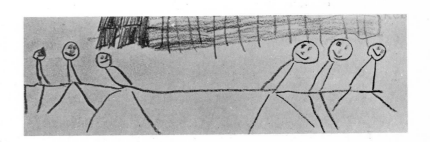

Long Horizontal Strip of Paper

At Dancing Class

Have you ever been in a dancing class? Was it ballet, tap, or creative dancing? How did you dress? What was on your feet? Was there music? Did you dance with a large group or with a small group of children? What sort of movements did you make? Did you dance on your toes? Did you move your arms, too? Did you bend your knees? How high can you stretch? How fast can you whirl around? What parts of your body can you push? Does dancing ever make you think of flying? Can you dance like an angry horse or a limp rag doll? Can you jump imaginary puddles, run quietly, take up as little space as possible, march like a tin soldier, kick very high, bend backwards and forwards, take a bow?

Draw your dancing class lined up on this long, long strip of paper. The children may all be doing the same thing or may be doing different things and may be dressed in the same or in different colors and kinds of costumes.

Tall Vertical Strip of Paper

WE CLIMBED A TALL, TALL LADDER

Did you ever play ball and suddenly lose the ball when it was thrown on the roof of the house or school building? Did you use a ladder to get it down?

Did you ever play in a tree house and have to climb a ladder to get up to the house? Were the rungs nailed to the tree or did the whole ladder lean against the tree?

Did your ever climb a ladder for any other reason?

How is a ladder made? Where do you put your hands? How do you climb it? Are both feet on the same step or do you put first one foot and then another on the rungs? Are your hands above your head pulling you up? Was the ladder you climbed made of wood or metal? Was it rough or smooth? Did you ever get a splinter from an old ladder?

If several children are climbing the ladder, who is first, second, third, fourth? Do you need to watch that the foot of the person above you doesn't hit you in the eye? Was the ladder leaning against the tree or house or was it straight up and down? Was the ladder steady or did it teeter and creak when you stepped on it as if it might break? Were you a little afraid as you got higher and higher? Did your heart pound a little? Were you dizzy? How did you climb down?

What kind of clothes were you and your friends wearing? What colors were they?

Draw yourself and at least two or three friends climbing a tall, tall ladder. Make the ladder start near the bottom of the paper and go up close to the top.

Before you start, think how you will arrange the children on the ladder and what colors you will choose for each part of your picture.

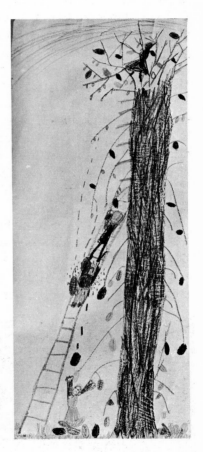

Tall Vertical Strip of Paper
(Suggested dimensions — 18″ x 8″ or 9″ x 24″)
WHEN I WENT INSIDE A TALL BUILDING

Have you ever gone inside a tall building? How many stories high was it? How high did you go? Do you remember how you felt when you got in the elevator or rode the escalator? Or did you walk up flights of stairs? What were you doing in the building? Were you going to see the doctor or dentist? Were you excited or frightened? Who was with you? Show me how you stood in the elevator or on the escalator. Did the elevator stop at each floor? Was there an attendant or did you push the buttons? What was on each floor? Did the elevator go fast and give you "butterflies" in your stomach? Were there windows in the building? What kind of building was it? Was it an office, a hospital, an apartment, a store, or something else? What did you see on each floor?

Draw a picture about when you rode an elevator or escalator or walked up flights of stairs in a tall, tall building. Make the first floor of your building start near the bottom of this tall thin strip of paper and make a lot of floors reaching to the top of the paper.

Tall Vertical Strip of Paper
WALKING ON STILTS

Stilts are "magic" sticks that can make a boy or girl grow into a very tall person as soon as he stands on them. Did you ever walk on stilts? Had someone made them for you? How far off the ground were you? How did you hold on? Where were your hands? How tall did you feel? Were you afraid of losing your balance and falling? Could you walk very fast? Were you as tall as your father or as tall as a house?

Did you ever see a clown wearing stilts? He probably had an especially long pair of trousers to wear over them so he looked like a tall thin giant. Can you imagine how long a leash the clown would need if he were leading a dog?

Draw yourself or a clown on stilts. Make the stilts start at the bottom of the paper and the head come all the way to the top of the paper.

Tall Vertical Strip of Paper
FAMILY OF BEARS CLIMBING A TALL REDWOOD TREE

How tall was the tallest tree you ever saw? Do you think you could climb it? Do you remember if the trunk was strong and sturdy? Was the bark rough?

Bears are good tree climbers. How are their feet different from yours? Why do you suppose bears climb trees? Could bears climb a tree if the tree had no branches? Did you ever see a bear climb a tree? How many feet does a bear use when he climbs a tree? Does he go up head first? Where does he sit when he wants to rest? Can bears walk out on a heavy branch? Could a bear hang by his two front legs and then drop to the ground?

How many cubs are usually in a family? (Two) Do you suppose the cubs are ever frightened? Who takes good care of them and teaches them to climb? Did you know that bears can walk on their two hind legs as well as on all four? How do you suppose a cub feels when he gets way up high and looks down? What would he see down below him? Do you suppose his mother might help him get down if he didn't know how?

What else might the mother, father, and cubs see while they were climbing a tall redwood tree besides branches and foliage? (Squirrels, chipmunks, knotholes, bees, honey, birds, bird nests, possibly other things.) What color will you make your bears? There are black bears, cinnamon bears, and of course grizzly bears. Are bears fat and shaggy? They do grow extra heavy coats of fur in winter. What sort of tails do they have? (Stub) What shape are their ears? (Small and round) What about their noses? (Rather long and pointed)

Draw a family of bears climbing a tall, tall redwood tree. Make your tree start at the bottom of this tall piece of paper and go all the way to the top. Make the trunk strong. The branches must be thick enough to hold all the family of bears, too. Leave room on the trunk and branches to show some of the bears climbing up and some resting and playing on a branch. You may use black and two colors.

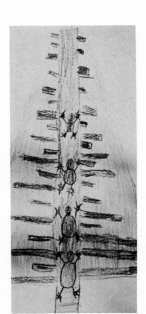

Circular Paper

(Suggested paper dimensions: 12 to 18″ diameter.)

A CARPET OF FLOWERS

There once was an enormous castle where a happy king and queen lived with their beautiful daughter, Gwendolyn. They had a bright garden where the sun danced on the flowers in the day and the moon smiled down gently at night. Many gardeners tended the flowers, and people came from far and near just to see all the many kinds of flowers that grew there. One day, the king announced that Princess Gwendolyn was to be married to the handsome Prince Andrew and that a prize would be given to the person in the Kingdom who would make the most beautiful carpet for the wedding ceremony. It was to be a circular or oval carpet made of flowers from the Royal Garden.

If you lived in that Kingdom, how would you design the carpet? Which of the royal flowers can you imagine? What colors would they be? What size? What shape? How would you arrange them?

After you are finished with the crayon design for the carpet, you might like to brush a thin water color wash over the paper. The color you use will fill in the background and won't cover the crayoned flowers as they are waxy, and the water will "resist" the flowers.

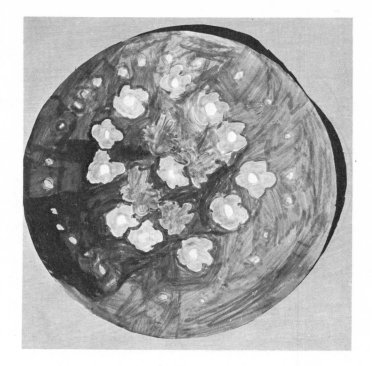

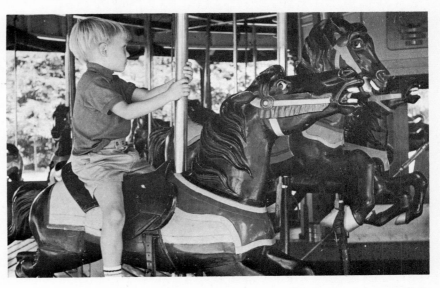

Circular Paper
WE ARE ON A MERRY-GO-ROUND

Up and down and around and around! What does that describe? Yes, a merry-go-round. Sometimes the horses (or other animals) are two or three layers deep. Are they all going in the same direction? Did you ever see a merry-go-round with benches between the horses? What are the poles for on a merry-go-round? Can you remember the special music that the calliope played? Some horses toss their heads, some race very fast, and others are prancing. What makes the horses so beautiful? What colors were they? How were their manes? What kind of saddles and decorations did they have on? Were there lights above you? What was in the middle of the merry-go-round?

How many horses can you draw on this circular paper? We will pretend that it is the base for the merry-go-round, and you may draw horses and riders all around it.

Circular Paper

WE ARE HOLDING HANDS IN A CIRCLE GAME

Farmer in the dell, Drop the handkerchief, Ring around the rosie, Three deep . . . . how are all these games alike? That's right . . . they are all played with the boys and girls holding hands and forming a large circle.

Let's all join hands and make a circle and walk around. Whose hands are you holding? Who is across from you? Are you holding your hands out very far?

Which game requires that someone be in the middle of the circle? Which game has someone chasing and running? Do you know any other games in which we must hold hands in a circle?

Draw a picture of a group of boys and girls holding hands in a circle. You may choose to put their feet on the outer rim of the circle and have their heads toward the middle; or you may prefer to put the heads near the outer rim and have the feet reaching toward the middle. How will the boys and girls be dressed? The circular paper will help you place the players in a ring.

Circular Paper

WE ARE ON A FERRIS WHEEL

How is a wagon wheel like a ferris wheel? What do you mean by spokes? What is in the center of a ferris wheel? Where are the seats arranged? How many seats are there on one? What is the shape of the seat? Did the seat you were in swing a bit and frighten you? How did it feel to be way, way up high? What could you see? Were you ever on a ferris wheel at night? How is it different from the day? Did you wave to someone below you? How did you hold on? Did anyone ride with you? Do you suppose the metal structure of a ferris wheel must be very strong? What supports it from the ground? Where is the motor that makes it run?

Draw a ferris wheel on this round paper. Show the seats and the people riding in them.

Chalk and Concrete

Colossal Giants

What other words can you use to say "big"? Large . . bulky . . huge . . mountainous . . enormous . . massive . . weighty . . Who is the largest person you know? How tall is he? Are you half as tall? Do you think anyone in the world could be larger? We're going to *Pretend* some people who are much more enor mous than any real living person. We're going to imagine *Giants*.

How do you think giants look? How much larger are they than normal people? How much larger do you suppose a giant's foot is than your foot? How many lengths of your leg would it take to make a giant's leg? Do you think you could climb up to his shoulder on a tall ladder? What do you think a giant might carry in his hands? Would you prefer to draw a friendly giant or a wicked one? What will you draw on your giant's head? Did you ever see a bushel basket? Perhaps that would be about the right size for a giant's hat. What sort of clothes would a giant be wearing? His buttons would probably be about the size of apples! Would his teeth be large, too? How large? What size would you make his eyes and ears? Would he have long hair or short? Can anyone imagine a lady giant? Draw an enormous giant with chalk on the concrete. (Patio, driveway, sidewalk, or play area)

Teacher's Note:

Plumber's chalk or a soft grade of white and colored chalk is best. Hosing the concrete easily erases the drawings.

Chalk and Concrete

DINOSAURS OR IMAGINARY MONSTERS

No one has ever seen a dinosaur because they lived about sixty million years ago before there were any people. "Dinosaur" means "terrible lizard." They weren't lizards, and not all of them were terrible. Five thousand kinds of dinosaurs inhabited the ancient world, and some were giant-sized. They were larger than elephants. Can you imagine the loud noises these creatures must have made? Can you imagine how many plants one of them had to eat each day?

We know how dinosaurs looked because we have found their bones and footprints in the rocks. Some had long necks and long tails. One had a duck-bill. One of the dinosaurs had teeth several inches long and walked on its hind legs and used the sharp claws on its front feet to kill other animals.

Some dinosaurs had strong armor to protect them from flesh-eating animals. One of them had a double row of plates down its back and sharp spikes on its tail. Instead of one or two horns, one of them had three horns and a frill of bone around its neck.

There aren't any dinosaurs today, but let's imagine how these monsters might look if they were living today. Who can make the hungriest, the angriest, the most wicked looking monster? Remember to draw him very large. Will his feet need to be huge? How will you draw his tail, his teeth, his horns, his spikes, his scaly hide? Will you draw your dinosaur eating grass, or eating another creature? Will he be wading in a swamp or eating plants? Will his mouth be open or shut?

Draw a huge dinosaur or an imaginary monster.

Chalk and Concrete

If a group of children are working cooperatively on this motivation, it is advisable for one of the older children to outline the basic "streets" in order that the entire group may relate their separate drawings to an organized whole.

A City or Village Street

Do you know what the word "crossroads" means? It is where two streets meet and cross each other. It makes four corners. Sometimes a street is curved. How shall we draw our street? How many corners shall we have? Some towns have a village square in the middle with a statue or benches and trees and a fountain. What sort of buildings will we need to make? We'll need a grocery store, a service station, drug store, post office. What else? Where will we draw the school? Who will draw the church? Will you draw any people walking down the street and going into the buildings or looking out of the windows? Could you draw children on bicycles or scooters or running down the sidewalk? Will you want to have trees, bushes, stop signs, traffic lights? How about some cars going down the street and perhaps an officer blowing his whistle? How about a fire truck, buses, trucks?

Where will the houses be? How will you make each house different? Will some be one story and some two? How about different shapes for windows and doors and shutters and different kinds of roofs? Where will you draw a flag?

Can you think of anything else to draw in our village?

Divergent Paths . . . Related Topics for . . .
POINT OF VIEW CHANGERS

Long horizontal strip of paper

A parade of elephants; Water skiing; A walk past the zoo cages; Cars and trucks bumper to bumper on the freeway; Walking along the boat dock; Riding through a spook tunnel; Wagon train crossing the prairie; Agnes Alligator; Wally Worm; Playing Snap-the-Whip; Playing Follow-the-Leader; Playing London Bridge Is Falling Down; Waiting at the bus stop; A street lined with houses

Tall vertical strip of paper

Men painting a tall building; Men washing windows on a tall building; Helping put up a TV antenna; Raising the American flag; A worker repairing a telephone line; Hibernating animals; Riding a ski lift; Astronauts in a rocket ship

Circular paper

Birds in a birdbath; Indians doing a rain dance; Looking into my fishbowl; A robin's nest; Maypole Dancers; Riding ponies in the park; My electric train; Race horses; Ice Skating on the pond

Chalk and concrete

Climbing the tallest tree in the world; A pirate ship and a treasure map; Many birds in a giant bush; Supersized bugs; Racing cars

Cluster Activities...
Murals and Other Projects

Cluster — group, crowd, body, crew, squad, gathering, congregation, conclave, team, committee

Cluster activities are those in which each child contributes something important and yet realizes that alone he could not have accomplished the task. In the elementary grades, these activities evolve principally around mural making.

All of the motivations described in this book lend themselves singly or in combination to cluster activities. The brisk verbal interchange should always sum up the items to be included in the mural, and from this list, each child makes his choice and works individually. A committee prepares the base for the mural by mapping out sky and foreground areas or whatever type of background the subject requires. A long strip of butcher paper is best processesd on the floor so that all the children may become cognitive of its entirety and will arrange their objects on it in relation to those of the other children.

The assembled mural is the most functional type for the young child's first mural making activities. Since each child makes his objects individually and later compiles them with the work of others, the concept of overlapping forms becomes meaningful. The relationship of distant and near objects are graphically illustrated by largeness and smallness, and a beginning awareness of perspective is realized.

Other projects such as roller T-V shows, miniature scenes, puppet shows, and accordian books are valuable cluster activities also and could be used with any of the motivational dialogues in this section.

Murals:

1. Crayon: Draw and color objects with crayons on white, manila, or colored paper. Cut them out. Assemble. Experiment with a variety of textures by using the crayon rubbing technique. (Hold paper over a surface such as a screen, corrugated cardboard, burlap, or some other material, and rub flat side of crayon over it.) Draw objects on the created surface, add detail, cut out, and assemble.

2. Paint: Paint objects on manila paper with tempera. Try dry brush, blotting with wadded paper towel, sponges, large and small brushes. Let dry and cut out. Assemble.

3. Cut Paper Two-Dimensional: Cut and tear and paste objects together using colored paper for all parts and details. Three-Dimensional: Use paper sculpture techniques such as curling, fringing, folding, and scoring to give the mural depth.

4. Finger Paint: Cut objects from paper upon which children have finger painted. An assortment of colors and textures are necessary for combining and adding details and parts.

5. Texture: Make objects from all sorts of colored and textured papers, yarn, string, toothpicks, bits of wire, seeds, shells, cotton, screen.

6. Printed: Each child makes his own inner tube print, potato print, or art gum print. By repeating his print several times on the surface, the mural acquires a grove of trees, a herd of cattle, a flock of birds, a row of flowers, or a group of clowns.

7. Cloth and Stitchery: Stretch length of burlap on wood frame. Use scraps of bright felt, cloth, yarn, string, and netting. Glue separate parts on burlap and add simple details with large stitches.

Other Projects

1. Roller T-V: Choose a topic with a chronological order, one that has a related sequence of events, or one that offers a wide range of variations. Each child chooses one phase or one part and draws or paints it. A long strip of butcher paper is fastened to a dowel stick or old broom handle and the individual pictures are pasted on the strip as it is rolled, the end of the paper being secured to another roller and the reel being held top and bottom in a cardboard carton in which a square or opening for the television "screen" has been cut.

2. Miniature scenes: Use a three-sided carton or box for projects requiring a monumental approach and use shoeboxes for smaller activities. All sorts of materials are used . . . sand, glass, foil, ribbon, sawdust, sponges, twigs, rocks, pipe cleaners, papier maché, cloth, string, wire, salt ceramic.

3. Puppet shows: For the youngest children, a simple form of puppetry involves filling a grocery bag with wads of newspaper and inserting a stick and taping it to the bag. This forms the puppet's head and features are added with colored paper, cloth, paint, yarn, steel wool, cotton. Another simple puppet form involves drawing figures on tag board and cutting them out. After decorating them with cut paper, bits of fabric, they are stapled to a tongue depressor or any short flat stick for a convenient handle. For older children, papier maché puppet heads are made with torn strips of newspaper dipped in a creamy wheat paste. These strips are wrapped snugly around the neck of a pop bottle which has been prepared by taping several layers of dry paper around the top in order that the finished head may be easily removed when it is dry. Features are exaggerated and stuck on with wads and strips of paper. Paint, yarn, cotton, and a mitten garment complete the puppet. Make

stage of large carton. Decorate it with paint, crepe paper, cloth. Make curtain, use spot light, and add music for background.

4. Accordion book: This approach is similar in concept to that of the roller movie except that the individual pictures are pasted to cardboard squares which are subsequently taped into an accordion-folded book.

Cluster Activities

At the Fair

Things we ride at the Fair . . .
. . . Who will make a picture about:
   Ferris wheels turning loads of people high in the sky
   Bright merry-go-grounds spinning dizzily to the tune of the piping calliope
   Whirling, speeding, noisy roller coasters
   Cable cars lifting passengers high overhead
   People lined up at the ticket booth
   The passenger touring train
   What else?

Things we eat at the Fair . . .
. . . Who will make a picture about:
Eating pink cotton candy
Eating popcorn
Buying snow cones at the stand
Buying hamburgers and hot dogs
Drinking lemonade through a straw
What else?

Things we do at the Fair . . .
. . . Who will make a picture about:
Trying to win a giant stuffed animal
Throwing rings, tossing coins,
Breaking balloons, throwing balls,
Shooting toy rifles
Jumping on the trampolines
Watching the trotting races
Buying balloons
Buying souvenir flags and toys on sticks

Things we see at the Fair . . .
. . . Who will make a picture about:
The fountain at the entrance gate
The floral display
The county display of animated figures
The bins and baskets of fruit and vege-
   tables with blue ribbons attached
The prize-winning cakes and pies
The stalls of sleek cows and pigs and
   woolly sheep and shining horses
The great crowds of people
What else?

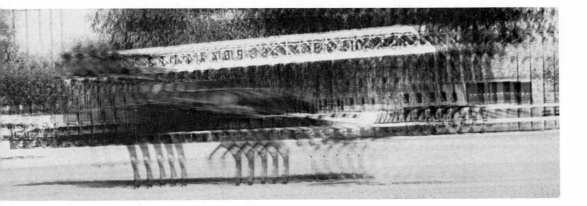

How will we group each part? Shall we use colored paper and cut and
paste, or shall we draw the parts with crayons or shall we use both?
How large will we make our background? Can we overlap things to show
that some things are in front of and behind other objects? Will the large
things be in the background? What colors will look gay and exciting?
Shall we put the faraway things near the top part of our mural?

Cluster Activities

BOATS AND SHIPS

Boats and ships carry people and products over the waters of rivers, bays, lakes, and oceans. Long ago, men probably used a log or raft to help them travel over the water.

Now we have many, many kinds of boats and ships. Who has ridden on a small boat . . . a large ship? Where did you go? Who has watched races, ships being loaded, fishing boats? What other kinds have you seen? Do you know the names of any of these vessels? How is a rowboat different from a sailboat? How is a sailboat like a clipper? Did you know that schooners, sloops, and brigs all have sails? Would you like to board the gangplank and take a cruise on an ocean liner? Did you ever look through a telescope at the wharf to see a cargo ship or a tugboat? Did you ever watch a ship loading cargo? How would you like to navigate a fishing boat? What kind of flag would you fly if you owned a yacht? How would you dress and what would you name your yacht?

How will we arrange our mural or miniature scene so that we can show a river and a lake or ocean? Will we need a wharf or

BLUE COAST, Feiringer
Courtesy of: The Columbus Gallery of Fine Arts
Columbus, Ohio

boat dock in the harbor? Who would like to make them? How about a pier? Shall we have a bridge? Who will make some of these things?

Ocean liners with tall steam stacks and many decks and portholes

Fishing boats with nets, ropes, cabins, and anchor

Racing boats with billowing sails

Sailboats tied up in rows

Tugboats pushing steamers

Motorboats churning up a trough of water followed by a water skier

Ferry boats taking cars and passengers across the bay

Old clipper ships complete with rigging, tall masts, gangplants, and a figurehead on the bow

Rowboats with someone pulling the oars

Yachts with captains on deck

Seagulls and clouds and sun

Think of the colors you will make the different parts of each boat or ship. Think of the general shape of each one. Think about the different parts and details that you will need to make or draw or cut out and paste onto your boat or ship. Which will be the largest ships? And which the smallest?

Cluster Activities

SUMMER FUN

Summer is a good time for exploring, discovering, making, doing, playing, or just plain loafing. What are some of the things we do in the summer?

Play on the beach . . .

. . . Some of you might want to make the part about children:

Building in the sand
Sailing toy boats
Finding odd things on the shore
Walking in the surf
Digging holes in the wet sand
Watching flashing minnows
Fishing with a pole
Making sand castles
Digging tunnels, bridges, and roads

Courtesy of: Continental Baking Company

Swim in the water . . .

   . . . Some of you can make the part about:

     Children floating in the pool

     Children diving off the spring board

     Someone diving off the high tower

     Someone floating in an inner tube

     Children playing with inflated plastic toys

     Someone diving off the side of the pool

     Swimmers racing

     The lifeguard in his high seat

     Children wading in the shallow water

Sunbathing . . .

   . . . .Some can make the part about people:

     Lying in the sun by the pool

     Lying on the sand by the lake or ocean

     Sitting under an umbrella

Playing in the trees . . .

   . . . Some of you will want to make the part about children:

     Building a tree house

     Climbing up the stairs or ladder to the tree house

     Climbing on the branches

     Swinging

What else do you do in the summer that we could draw and assemble in our mural?

TEACHER'S NOTE

    Any of the themes that appeal to the particular group of children can be expanded. The summer fun will vary according to the geographical location and the experiences of the children.

CERAMIC OX, T'ang Dynasty
Courtesy of: E. B. Crocker Art Gallery
Sacramento, California

Cluster Activities
AT THE FARM

Would you like to live on a farm? Did you ever visit a farm? What buildings are needed to carry on all the activities of farm life? What machines are used? What animals do many farms have? If you would ever visit a farm, which animals would you like to feed? Did you ever feel a pony's nose? Did you ever climb on a farm fence? What kind of a house does a chicken live in? How is a barn shaped? Is it larger than the house? What is in it? Where is hay kept? Where do the pigs stay? Did you ever see a duck pond on a farm? What colors are cows? How are their ears different from a horse's? How is a cow's tail different from a horse's? How are the hoofs of the two animals different? Did you ever see a calf nursing? How many piglets do you suppose a sow has? What colors are sheep? How large is a sheep compared to a horse? Shall we make some goats for our mural? Which animal might be spotted? How many different colors of hens and roosters have

you seen? What color are baby chicks? Do you know the different noises farm animals make? Did you ever watch farm animals chew and munch and peck their food? Did you ever smell freshly cut hay? What else would you see on a farm?

Some things to make are:

    The barn
    The silo
    The farmer and his family
    The hired hands
    The chicken house
    The pen for the pigs
    The pond for the ducks
    The pasture and fence
    The farm house
    The trees
    The road and gate
    The mailbox
    The vegetable garden
    The orchard
    The tractors and plows

Some animals to make are:

    Cows and calves
    Horses and colts
    Mules
    Donkeys
    Sheep
    Lambs
    Goats
    Pigs
    Ducks
    Geëse
    Chickens
    Dogs
    Cats
    Turkeys

Divergent Paths . . . Related Topics for . . .
CLUSTER ACTIVITIES

At the ski run; On our playground; At the train station; A trip to outer space; At the airport; In the jungle; At the shopping center; Christmas Eve in our town; Along the River; Scout Camp; A royal Kingdom.